GOD'S MAN IN THE MARKET-PLACE

PLACE

*The Story of
Herbert J. Taylor*

■ PAUL H. HEIDEBRECHT

INTERVARSITY PRESS
DOWNERS GROVE, ILLINOIS 60515

© 1990 by Christian Workers Foundation

InterVarsity Press is the book-publishing division of InterVarsity Christian Fellowship, a student movement active on campus at hundreds of universities, colleges and schools of nursing in the United States of America, and a member movement of the International Fellowship of Evangelical Students. For information about local and regional activities, write Public Relations Dept., InterVarsity Christian Fellowship, 6400 Schroeder Rd., P.O. Box 7895, Madison, WI 53707-7895.

All Scripture quotations in this publication are from the Holy Bible, New International Version. Copyright © 1973, 1978, International Bible Society. Used by permission of Zondervan Bible Publishers.

Cover illustration: Carlos Vergara

ISBN 0-8308-1733-6

Printed in the United States of America

Library of Congress Cataloging-in-Publication Data

Heidebrecht, Paul Henry, 1950-
    God's man in the marketplace: the story of Herbert J. Taylor/
Paul Heidebrecht.
        p.   cm.
    Includes bibliographical references.
    ISBN 0-8308-1733-6
    1. Taylor, Herbert John, 1893-1978. 2. Christian biography—
United States. 3. Businessmen—United States—Biography.
4. Rotary International—Presidents—Biography.   I. Title.
BR1725.T28H45   1990
267'.13'092—dc20
[B]   90-37145
                                                  CIP

13   12   11   10   9   8   7   6   5   4   3   2   1
99   98   97   96   95   94   93   92   91   90

To Gloria Taylor
who is as charming and beautiful
as she was when she
first met Herb Taylor.

Preface

One summer, when I was a teen-ager, I cut grass in an old cemetery. I became familiar with the hundreds of tombstones standing in quiet rows among the trees. I sensed there were intriguing stories behind the names engraved in stone, but I could only imagine what they might be.

Who still remembers this person? I often wondered as I paused beside a grave. And what's worth remembering about this man or woman? What makes any of these people significant?

These same questions still linger with me today. I am convinced that every person's life is valuable enough to remember; many are sufficiently interesting to re-tell to later generations. I believe this because every person is a unique creation of God.

But how will any person's life and accomplishments be captured for others to appreciate? One way is for biographers and historians to faithfully record the events of an individual's life and respectfully probe the inner dimensions of his or her thoughts and emotions. Such people are storytellers, collectors of memories, conveyors of a past that still speaks to the present. Perhaps my teen-age cemetery musings were a signal of a future calling to just this kind of task. In any case, I am honored to tell the story of Herbert J. Taylor, a man whom I never met, yet one in whose tracks I have followed for several years.

Herb Taylor was an entrepreneur in the finest sense of that word. He was a businessman who took ethics seriously, an executive who displayed a genuine interest in the people he employed and the customers he served. Though widely acclaimed as a business success story, his company, Club Aluminum of Chicago, experienced failures and disappointments, but none of these really tarnish his reputation as much as endear him to those who knew him.

Taylor was also an ordinary Christian layman, motivated by a profound, though simple, piety, who emerged as a powerful leader in the evangelical subculture in the United States. He was a rare human being, loved and admired by hundreds if not thousands of people. He was disliked by almost no one.

I am not the first person to write about Taylor's life. Robert Walker, a close friend and protégé of Taylor, was the editor behind Taylor's autobiography *God Has a Plan for You* (Revell). Walker encouraged me and gave me the benefit of his warm memories.

There were others who talked freely and fondly of Taylor: daughter and son-in-law Beverly and Allen Mathis; daughter and son-in-law Ramona and Bob Lockhart; Charlie Cecil and Ken Johnston, both of whom were hired by Taylor and who became Club Aluminum executives. To each of these persons I am indebted. A special treat for me was to speak with Mrs. Gloria Taylor, a woman who complemented her husband in many ways while retaining her own sparkle and independent character.

Taylor's personal papers and his Club Aluminum files are properly stored and capably managed by the staff of the Billy Graham Center Archives where I spent many hours. Bob Schuster, Paul Erickson and Lannae Graham deserve thanks for all the fine work they do.

Finally, I wish to thank Pete Hammond of Marketplace and Allen Mathis of the Christian Worker's Foundation for asking me to write this biography. I hope and pray that I have fulfilled their hopes for this book.

Introduction

Herbert Taylor was a hero to many of his contemporaries. He was celebrated as a Christian who had succeeded in business without compromising his moral principles. Indeed, the code of ethics he developed for his company was credited for his phenomenal success in restoring the debt-ridden firm he took over during the Depression. He was idolized by his fellow Rotarians for countless deeds of service, generosity and goodwill, which earned him the position of Rotary International's president during its Golden Anniversary year in 1955. Evangelical leaders joined in with paeans of praise for the vision and organizational savvy which launched at least five parachurch youth ministries, a theological seminary and numerous evangelistic campaigns.

But reciting accomplishments is for banquets and funerals. Understanding the real Herbert Taylor requires a more penetrating look into his career, his relationships and the ideas which he left behind embedded in speeches, letters and articles. This kind of close examination reveals a more genuine human being, a man whose efforts to practice his faith didn't always come easily. Like anyone else, he faced social and economic conditions to which he had to respond. He was not in total control of his destiny, though he pursued definite goals with concentrated devotion. The circumstances in which he found himself during his business career shaped the choices he made. These circumstances need to be outlined if we are to appreciate the true character of this man.

Boom, Bust, Boom

Taylor's five decades of activity as a corporate executive encompassed both lean and prosperous years. He was expected to turn a profit during the 1930s when bankruptcies were as common as soup lines and dust storms. When the United States entered World War II in 1941, he was forced into the complete curtailment of the production of aluminum, the thing on which his entire business relied; a similar, less severe restriction was imposed again during the Korean War in the early 1950s. Stiff competition from other cookware manufacturers made even the best years demanding.

The story of Taylor's Club Aluminum is fairly typical of the way many American companies grew. They began in the exciting years around the turn of the century, when the United States became a world economic power. The abundance of cheap unskilled labor, the invention of mass-production technology and the availability of vast sums of capital combined to fuel tremendous growth in manufacturing. Business boomed through the 1920s as cars, radios, telephones and numerous household appliances became available to the middle-class customer.

The stock-market crash of 1929 burst the bubble and plunged the nation into a decade of widespread unemployment and meager profits. The war ended the Depression for all practical purposes as industry was harnessed for the production of weapons and materiel. After the war, the U.S. economy took off and didn't stop expanding until the 1970s. An entire generation of Americans was raised in this prosperity and given an education unparalleled in previous generations. A consumer society sprang up to which companies had to respond in order to survive.

Often, corporate giants swallowed up the smaller fish in the pond. In the cookware industry, for example, there were dozens of companies competing for a share of the same market during the 1930s and 40s; by the 70s, there were only a handful, each of them having absorbed various smaller firms. In fact, Club Aluminum now belongs to one of its former competitors.

The perception of businessmen in American culture during the first part of this century has alternated between heroes on one hand and villains on the other. When Taylor went to work for an Oklahoma oil company in 1919, businessmen were held in high esteem and often played critical roles as civic leaders. During the Depression, their stock plummeted as the public blamed their greediness for the economy's collapse. As the century wore on, the businessman became invisible, a faceless bureaucrat in a huge conglomerate, an "organization man" who sacrificed his personal identity to move up the corporate ladder.

In more recent years, the flamboyant, ruthless executive has re-emerged. Wall Street tycoons and Fortune 500 executives have captured the public imagination, though few admire them. In fact, most of us suspect they have no moral scruples keeping them from accumulating huge profits. Even the phrase "business ethics" has become a joke for its apparent contradiction in terms.

Today Herbert Taylor may seem like an anachronism. He really believed that getting people—whether company managers, union contract negotiators, or even high-school students—to ask four simple questions (such as, "Is it fair to all concerned?") could actually change their behavior. He refused to sell his company to any potential buyers who would not accept his ethical standards or who might treat his employees unfairly. He even scrutinized the advertising copy for company products to be sure their claims were accurate. His Christian ethics not only affected his own company; he had an influence throughout the cookware industry. His competitors knew him and admired him for his consistent standards.

In many ways, Taylor was an old-fashioned businessman who treated his employees like family members. He relied on the traditional virtues of hard work, enthusiasm, a positive attitude and ingenuity rather than the insights of management theory and marketing studies—which younger executives tried to press on him. He resisted giving company employees too many fringe benefits, preferring to let them work for incentives and bonuses.

There is no one management style that fits all companies. Certainly, Taylor's gentle paternalism was not inappropriate for the hard years of the 1930s and 40s. Those were, by far, his best years. Under adverse conditions, he built his company into a leading aluminum-cookware distributor.

From Protestants to Evangelicals
If the business climate exploded during Taylor's years as CEO of Club Aluminum, so did the religious world in which he operated. What he knew as a boy differed greatly from the church scene of his retirement years.

In 1893, when Taylor was born, to be an American was to be Protestant, generally speaking. The Protestant denominations, which were fairly orthodox, conservative and Bible-believing, controlled American culture. Catholics and Jews were tolerated but had little influence; the Blacks living in the South and the millions of Eastern European immigrants crowded into big-city slums were ignored, if not exploited. Protestant families could assume that public schools, government, newspapers and popular literature would reinforce their religious beliefs and values, not undermine them.

But during the 1920s and 30s, American society became more secular and more religiously diverse. Intellectuals shed their religious pasts and espoused a pragmatic, humanistic philosophy of life. While most people still professed a belief in God, increasing numbers lived as if he didn't exist. Religion became a private matter, not to be discussed in polite circles or debated in public forums.

The advances of scientific knowledge made much of religion obsolete in the minds of many Americans; the primary value of religion was in promoting morals. Even though the much-publicized Scopes Trial in 1925 ruled against the teaching of evolution, fundamentalist Christianity lost all credibility and was laughed from the stage. The major Protestant denominations made their peace with the demands of modern society by abandoning doctrines which seemed unreasonable or unscientific. The result was that the Protestant community was permanently divided between conservatives and liberals, a separation that would affect Taylor in personal ways throughout his life.

Meanwhile, Catholics and Jews asserted their own claims to be heard and respected. The sheer size of the Catholic population made them a formidable force in urban politics. Though smaller in numbers, Jews excelled culturally and in the business world. By the mid-50s, sociologist Will Herberg was able to describe an American civil religion that had three tributaries: Protestant, Catholic and Jewish. Not surprisingly, Taylor appealed to these same three traditions whenever he spoke of belief in God among Rotarians. This did not lessen his desire that Catholics and Jews be converted to evangelical Protestantism; at the same time, he acknowledged their legitimate place on the American religious scene.

Like many older Protestants in the post-World War II era, Taylor realized that aggressive leadership by evangelicals was essential if their cultural values were to be maintained. He was not reactionary, like some fundamentalists who withdrew into their own enclaves while waiting for judgment to fall on America.

Rather, he relished the opportunity to apply new methods of evangelism among teen-agers and college students, to capitalize on dynamic young evangelists like Billy Graham, and to permeate American society with Christian values by means of Bible distribution and codes of ethics. Taylor was a pio-

neer and represented the new evangelicals who, after World
War II, set aside the restrictive elements of the fundamentalist heritage and became a powerful force on the American
religious scene in the 70s and 80s.

Broadcasting Your Message

The world grew smaller during Taylor's lifetime. He left behind the town of his childhood, a village that typified rural
America of the last century—remote, isolated, quaint, secure.
Chicago became his home, a sprawling metropolis known for
its gang warfare, racial strife, machine politics, manufacturing muscle and ugly poverty. Taylor saw Chicago at its best
and its worst.

But it was not just the urbanization of America that transformed Taylor's generation; it was also the creation of one
common culture by means of radio and television which
reached into every home. The events that shook the world
invaded the living room as they were happening. America
became one vast audience, whether for Franklin Delano
Roosevelt's fireside chats, or Jack Benny's humor or Ed Sul-
livan's guest talent.

Unlike the media in other parts of the world, American
broadcasting was a commercial vehicle from the very beginning. It was a means for enterprising businessmen to advertise their products. It was not unusual for the sponsors to
prepare the programs. This was the case when Taylor started
his Club Time radio broadcast in 1947 in which the favorite
hymns of famous personalities were sung.

Mass communications expanded people's horizons. It was
possible to preach to millions over the air waves, not just
thousands in an auditorium. It was possible to sell to every

household in America, not just to those individuals who entered a particular store. Taylor learned to think on a grand scale, to expect great things of God, to dream about changing a whole society.

Whatever Happened to Cooking?

Taylor also grew up in a world in which men and women had defined their roles and accepted the distinctions between them. That world also changed during his career in ways that impacted his business.

For obvious reasons, the cookware industry has always catered to housewives. It advertised its products to discerning women looking for efficiency in food preparation, as well as safety and the opportunity to enhance their culinary skills. The success of the industry was built on the assumption that women found their fulfillment in being first-rate homemakers. Taylor understood this principle from his earliest years with Club Aluminum and geared all his marketing efforts to appeal to the sophisticated woman in the home. He corresponded with hundreds of housewives over the years, answering complaints, replacing broken parts and giving away samples in exchange for evaluations. His marketing savvy and customer-service orientation enabled him to make the most of his opportunities.

But as married women entered the work force and family living patterns changed in the 60s and 70s, cooking as an art and a skill declined in value. There wasn't time for extensive meal preparation on a daily basis. More meals were eaten in restaurants or heated up in ovens. People did not stop buying pots and pans, but the market for such products had changed dramatically.

Taylor on the Grid

All of these factors demonstrate that Taylor was a man of his time. He was a pioneer in the field of merchandising, an innovator in manufacturing with metals, a motivator of human beings. As the years went by, he was overtaken by others with similar qualities, but more energy and new knowledge. By the mid-50s, he had made his distinct contribution to the industry and chose to pursue other goals he had set for himself. Not only had he made the most of the career he chose, but he impacted the workplace with his Christian values and found a way to serve God through his company.

In his book *Your Work Matters to God* (Navpress, 1988), Doug Sherman describes three common but inadequate views of work held by Christians in North America.

One is the "secular" view. God has nothing to do with your job or career; work is an end in itself, a means to personal fulfillment, the cause to which a person sacrifices everything in order to succeed. These values contradict the priorities of Christianity, but many Christians, have bought into them anyway, becoming slaves to their work.

A second view distinguishes between work that is spiritual and pleasing to God and work that is ordinary and insignificant in God's sight. In the first category, we place missionaries, pastors and Christian workers; in the second, all the occupations that most laypeople pursue. Obviously, this represents a false dichotomy between sacred and secular, but it is very common among evangelical Christians who are eager to do the Lord's will. The unfortunate result is that it tells average laypeople that they are not very important to God because they settled for God's second best.

A third view, according to Sherman, looks at all work as a

context for evangelism. A job is worthwhile if it affords opportunity to witness to non-Christians. The work itself is not
that important. The only purpose in life is to obey the Great
Commission. Though Sherman is anxious to not downgrade
personal evangelism, he criticizes this view because it pro-
motes a less-than-biblical view of work, even to the point of
overlooking unethical and irresponsible activities by a company in which a Christian works.

What is a biblical view of work? Simply this, says Sherman:
Work matters to God because God is a worker, and he created us to be workers. Through our work, we demonstrate our
love for God, we serve Christ as Lord, and we meet the needs
of other people, including our families. Our work becomes
God's work. When we work his way, we bring glory to him.

To evaluate Herbert Taylor's career as a cookware salesman against Sherman's grid provides significant insights into
the role of Christians in the marketplace. To a certain degree,
Taylor represents Sherman's description of a biblical view of
work, though at times he clearly entertained both the second
and third views. Taylor earnestly believed that God was a
factor in his work and that the relationships and work habits
of a company could be directed toward the honor of God.
Taylor attempted to translate the standards of the Bible into
practical guidelines for business practice; because they were
from God, he was convinced they would produce good results.

As the story of Taylor's life unfolds in the following chapters, the model of "marketplace faith" he represents will
emerge. His personality and unique characteristics will also
appear. It will be hard to pigeonhole him or make too many
generalizations about him. Certainly, his story will provide a
compelling and attractive example to follow.

1

Early Years

Herbert Taylor was born on April 18, 1893, in Pickford, Michigan, a small town of some 300 residents located in the logging territory of the Upper Peninsula. He was the third of seven children born to Frank and Martha Ellen Taylor. His boyhood was typical of rural American children at the turn of the century. Public school, chores, fishing and church added up to a rich, satisfying life for almost any youngster.

Undoubtedly, Taylor acquired many of his entrepreneurial instincts and abilities from his father. The older Taylor practically ran the town. He established the telephone company and the electric company while running a lumber-supply firm, a bank and a dairy. He encouraged his children to work; as they grew older, he turned over various companies to them to manage.

The young Herbert responded eagerly to his father's challenge. His first business venture was raising sheep. By selling the wool and the sheep themselves, he was able to save enough money for school. In the frigid climate of northern Michigan, he often brought the lambs indoors to feed and protect them. The boy also sold advertising for the dairy. His whirlwind pace of busy activity was well underway even before he reached high school, and it continued for the rest of his life. So did his penchant for dabbling in many enterprises at the same time.

His most life-changing moment occurred when Herbert was sixteen years old. Every spring traveling evangelists made their appearances at the Methodist church in Pickford where the Taylor family attended. At one revival service, Taylor went forward and confessed Christ as his Savior. "The most wonderful thing happened to me on that occasion," he told audiences later. That experience was the official beginning of his relationship with God.

Pickford had no high school so Taylor moved to Sault Ste. Marie, a small city twenty-five miles away, where he boarded and earned his way through school. For a period of time, he worked for Western Union as a telegraph operator. One particular evening, while on duty at Soo Junction, a freight train pulled in. The conductor informed the young Taylor that it was picking up some cars in the yard and would return shortly. Meanwhile, the train dispatcher sent in an order for that freight train to pull off the track forty miles ahead to allow another train through. Taylor signaled back that everything was clear, which was not exactly the truth—he had not communicated anything to the conductor of the freight train. When the freight train didn't return, the frantic Taylor realized that the conductor might have changed his mind and gone ahead without returning. Herbert ran into the rainy night and chased down the freight train, helping to avert an almost certain train crash. It was a lesson about telling the truth which he never forgot.

Eager College Student

Taylor's next stop was Northwestern University in Chicago, a school then affiliated with the Methodist denomination. He chose to attend Northwestern (rather than the University of Chicago where he had already been accepted) primarily because of the warm reception he received at one of its fraternity houses. Yet Taylor continued to work his way through school by selling typewriters, working for a telegraph company and writing sports news for two Chicago newspapers (using the telegraph to wire his stories before the regular reporters had their stories written). He was also the business manager of the college yearbook, responsible for selling advertising space.

Taylor's formula for success in college was organization. "I carried a notebook and scheduled every hour of every day for a week in advance," he said. "The schedule allowed an average of about six hours of sleep a night, but I stuck to it."

On that schedule, however, was time to date a fourteen-year-old high-school girl, Gloria Forbrich, who later distinguished herself at Northwestern as a vocal soloist. Taylor, who was seven years older, charmed her and her parents, and he became a regular visitor in their home. The Forbrich family had a rich ancestry. Among Gloria's forebears were Revolutionary War hero Ethan Allen and temperance and women's suffrage activist Francis Willard.

But marriage had to wait. The United States' resistance to entering World War I had broken down. The role of the YMCA in the war effort became particularly significant: it raised millions of dollars to provide relief in the form of food and clothing to refugees, especially in Belgium. It also provided entertainment, recreation, worship and even a postal service for the troops. When Taylor graduated from Northwestern in 1917, he volunteered to work with the YMCA in France.

When the United States officially declared war against Germany, Taylor immediately signed up with the navy. He was commissioned as a lieutenant and assigned to the Naval Supply Department. When the war ended in November 1918, Taylor was asked to remain in France with the YMCA in an administrative post, which he held for almost another year.

Throughout the war, Taylor and his sweetheart corresponded regularly, even numbering the letters they exchanged (the total was over a thousand, all of which were faithfully preserved by Gloria). In 1919 Taylor returned home, and within a month he and Gloria were married. Before the year had ended, the two had moved to Paul's Valley, Oklahoma, where Taylor had taken a job with the Sinclair Oil Company, serving as assistant manager for a pipeline station then under construction. Within a year, he decided to go into business for himself as a lease broker for oil exploration and as an insurance salesman.

Taylor had the right attitude for selling. He believed it was the best way to make a living and recommended it to anyone who asked him for advice. For him, selling was not merely "handing over merchandise for money."

"There's more to it than that," he said. "I'm talking about

selling yourself, your ideas and ideals, the basic things you believe in. Direct selling, meeting people face to face in their homes with their children, will teach you more about them than you'll ever find out in almost any other profession. Once you understand people's needs and desires—spiritual as well as physical—you learn about another great secret of successful living: that being of service to others and thinking of them primarily instead of yourself is the surest way to make good."

Some of his experiences in Paul's Valley confirmed these ideas about selling. The most dramatic was a family on the verge of divorce. Taylor showed up at the door as the sheriff was leaving after serving a summons to the husband of the estranged wife. Taylor started to leave, then returned to console the husband and urge him to be reconciled with his wife. Taylor then went to speak with the woman, brought her home to her family and sold an oil lease on the man's property—all in one day!

Taylor discovered how to sell a life insurance policy without ever using the words "life insurance." Because of a customer's aversion to the whole idea, and to salesmen in general, Taylor changed his strategy. "I realized that first finding out what the other fellow's needs are is the way to sell."

If people refused to buy insurance, Taylor determined not to blame them. He preferred to blame himself for not figuring out the best way to sell to these people. Their resistance became a problem to be solved. Taylor often credited Gloria for teaching him this lesson of not blaming the customer. "She told me it was my job to sell the product," he said. "If I couldn't sell a customer, it was up to me to find a different way."

Taylor soon emerged as a leading businessman in the community; he spearheaded the Chamber of Commerce's drive for paved roads in the county and was nicknamed "Sign-'em-Up Taylor" because of his aggressive petition campaign. He also raised funds for construction of a new hotel for the town and acquired stock in several other local companies.

It was also in Paul's Valley where Taylor first became involved with the Rotary Club, a public-service organization begun in Chicago in 1905, which had 758 chapters around the world by 1921. In the 1920s, Rotary was ridiculed by such critics as Sinclair Lewis and H. L. Mencken for its image as a small-town, simple-minded businessmen's lunch with a pep-rally atmosphere. In later years, it was to become a massive network of dedicated middle-class leaders engaged in building hospitals, sponsoring foreign students and establishing vocational schools for youth around the world. Taylor helped to start a Rotary Club in Paul's Valley and through it initiated a variety of projects for the benefit of local youth, including a Boy Scout troop and high-school clubs.

After five years in Oklahoma, Taylor and his wife decided to return to Chicago, where he was hired to be an executive in training with the Jewel Tea Company. He began as a traveling salesman, opening up new territory for the regular salesmen who supplied customers' homes with various groceries.

Coffee and tea companies sold their products in this way, usually with wagons stocked with a variety of products. Independent peddlers were used at first, especially in rural areas, but eventually the companies took over the routes themselves. Many of these same companies, such as National,

Kroger and A&P, carried many other types of food besides tea and coffee; in large urban areas, they opened stores and gradually phased out of the wagon sales. Jewel was one of the larger direct-sales tea companies in the United States. Later, in the 1930s, it became one of the major retail grocery chains in the country. Taylor enjoyed the challenge of this competitive business. Door-to-door selling really puts a person to the test, he claimed. "It acquaints him with human nature, develops initiative, the courage to face people, the ability to think fast, and an understanding of how to help others."

Taylor did well. He became Jewel's office manager and in 1926, assistant to the president, M. H. Karker. Karker appreciated his young executive immensely (Karker had been Taylor's commanding officer in the navy) and made him a vice president and director in 1928. Taylor even published two booklets with the American Management Association about office management. He was clearly a man on the rise in the corporate world.

Family Traditions

By this time, Gloria Taylor had given birth to two daughters, Beverly and Ramona. Even though he left much of the child-rearing to Gloria, Taylor always showed an interest in the activities of his daughters. He enjoyed playing table games with them, bringing them gifts back from his trips, or attending their piano, dance and drama recitals. Often Taylor took his family with him on trips, especially to Rotary conventions. He delighted in taking movies or slides of his children.

At the same time, Taylor encouraged Gloria to pursue her musical interests. She resumed her voice lessons with the goal of singing in operas and eventually performed semi-professionally; during her life she was able to use her talent in various ministry situations as well. She almost upstaged her husband at Rotary gatherings where she was treated like royalty.

The Taylor home was a quiet, controlled, secure environment. Both daughters state that they cannot remember even one occasion when their father raised his voice in anger or frustration. He was a gentle, self-controlled man whose example was the predominant form of communicating values and truth. "You could see my parents' love for the Lord," said Beverly. "It was very evident." Herbert did not conduct a daily family devotional, though he prayed at every meal and memorized Scripture on his own, eventually spending an hour a day in personal Bible reading.

Herbert and Gloria taught a high-school Sunday-school class for more than twenty-five years; both Beverly and Ramona were students in their parents' class. Beverly met her future husband in the class as well.

"I don't remember a lot of content from that class," admits Ramona, "but I know that it was responsible for my gravitating toward the Bible later in life." During some years, there were over eighty teen-agers enrolled in the class. After being together for an opening exercise, Taylor taught the boys and Gloria the girls. One former student was Donald Hoke, a leader among American evangelicals, who became a missionary to Japan and founded Tokyo Christian College. Taylor corresponded with many of his former students in later years.

Taylor was a formal man, wearing a suit and tie even when he was at home. Sundays were observed in a rather conservative Methodist tradition. He avoided shopping on Sundays and any type of paid entertainment. Instead, the family often spent the day visiting relatives in the Chicago area, especially the country estate of Estellene and Milton Holloway (of Holloway Candies), Gloria's sister and brother-in-law. They also spent countless Sundays with Gloria's other sister, Eloise, and her husband, Elliot Youngberg.

Yet Taylor was not a legalist and rarely criticized how other people practiced their faith. He had his own convictions and lived by them. This was the case with alcohol. Taylor was a strict teetotaller, as an example for youth, never serving liquor in his home and always drinking a Coke at dinners where cocktails were served.

The Taylors took up residence in Park Ridge, a suburb northwest of Chicago. There they became members of the First Methodist Church. And Taylor remained loyal to his denomination to the end. Sunday-school class became an evangelical outpost in the church. Taylor was also a trustee and the spark plug of the adult-fellowship group. The stained-glass windows of this historic church were contributed by Taylor in memory of his mother.

As the 1920s drew to a close, Taylor and his family were comfortably established in a promising business career, an excellent neighborhood and a traditional church. But a dramatic change was around the corner.

2

Beginnings: Club Aluminum

The stock-market crash of 1929 sent shock waves through the American business community and triggered one of the longest, most devastating, economic recessions in the nation's history. Thousands of companies were forced to close their doors; even more teetered on the brink of disaster.

One of those companies on the verge of collapse was the Club Aluminum Utensil Company, a Chicago-based firm that specialized in "waterless cookware," then a revolutionary idea. Club sold its products through home demonstrations in which salesmen actually prepared meals with Club cookware at home parties. The company had grown rapidly during the 1920s, but because of poor management, it had accumulated a sizable debt even before Wall Street took its plunge. With creditors "breathing down their necks," the board of directors went looking for help.

They found it at the Continental National Bank, which persuaded Maurice Karker and the Jewel Tea Company to offer the services of Herbert Taylor on a half-time basis. This rather unusual arrangement of leasing an executive (rather than buying out the ailing company) proved to be a creative solution. Taylor had distinguished himself at Jewel in merchandising and manufacturing, two areas that Club Aluminum was involved in with little success. The bank's interest in keeping such a company afloat was obvious. There were also 250 jobs at stake at the Club headquarters, in addition to hundreds of salesmen across the country.

Taylor was made president of Club Aluminum for a period of three years, while still retaining his position as executive vice president of Jewel. He drew a small salary and the promise of a percentage of the company's earnings. His job was clear, but daunting: reorganize the management, cut expenses, eliminate the huge inventory and make the company profitable again. Several other Jewel employees went with Taylor on this rescue mission, but no further agreements were made between the companies.

It didn't take long for Taylor to discover that Club Aluminum was in worse shape than anyone realized. There were several lawsuits against the company which had to be settled. When all the debts were added up, Club Aluminum was $400,000 in the red, a staggering amount in the early years of the Depression. In addition to selling cookware house-to-house, Club's salesmen were also peddling radio sets, health lamps, electric massagers and vacuum cleaners. None of these product lines were generating adequate income.

However, Taylor sensed that one of Club Aluminum's major problems was its so-called party plan, or home-luncheon demonstrations. This merchandising strategy had produced tremendous success years before—more than five million homes in the United States had Club Aluminum cookware in their kitchens, a remarkable accomplishment for a company only in business since 1923—but now it was dragging the company down.

Ironically, it was a Methodist preacher who started the business. Struggling to earn his way through seminary in the early 1920s, W. A. Burnette sold cookware door to door. He soon found his true calling when the Monarch Aluminum Ware Company in Cleveland gave him the right to sell their cast-aluminum cookware and small appliances. Burnette devised the idea of hosting a meal in a customer's home to which friends and neighbors were invited. The rather dramatic demonstration of waterless cooking and the easy credit terms he offered produced enormous sales.

Within a few years, Club Aluminum had a huge team of salesmen across the country who were known for their high-pressure tactics. The fact that they earned a forty-per-cent commission on a set of cooking utensils which sold for $250 was all the incentive they needed. Burnette's success led to the introduction of other cast-aluminum products, such as vacuum cleaners, which were sold in a similar manner.

Monarch was by no means the only aluminum cookware manufacturer; in 1923, there were over thirty-five firms, most of them only a few years old, trying to capture the potential of this new metal. Monarch had been founded in 1913 by Raymond Deutsch who manufactured cookware and vacuum-cleaner parts by sand-casting aluminum. In 1920, he developed a permanent-mold process which resulted in heavy, one-piece utensils without seams and a smooth, rounded surface. Cast aluminum, as it was called, was particularly suitable for large pots, griddles, Dutch ovens and pressure cookers.

Aluminum cookware was not without its problems. First, it was expensive. Originally a metal that was treated like gold and priced even higher, aluminum was first produced in the United States in 1886 by Charles Hall, a young Pennsylvania inventor. Hall discovered how to separate aluminum through an electrolytic process. With financial backing he began the Pittsburgh Reduction Company, later known as the Aluminum Company of America, or Alcoa.

Cooking utensils were some of the first products to be made with aluminum. Because aluminum cost as much as $2.25 a pound in 1890, these utensils were still expensive for the average housewife. The advantages of aluminum were its long-term durability, its ability to conduct heat evenly, and its rustproof quality. The heavy aluminum pots and pans were called waterless because they transmitted heat evenly, not requiring water to prevent food from burning. Salesmen also pointed out that cooking with water boiled off valuable ingredients.

When the Depression hit, the steep price of aluminum cookware became a serious liability. At Club Aluminum in 1930, Taylor was faced with the challenge of reducing a huge stock of pots and pans at a severely reduced profit margin.

To make matters worse, aluminum utensils had developed a bad reputation in some circles. Though aluminum did not rust, it did tend to discolor and tarnish, usually because of the alkalies in certain foods. Alkalies also caused pitting in the metal in the form of tiny holes in which food particles lodged if the cookware was not properly cleaned.

While the manufacturers worked to solve these problems, a more serious charge was made in the 1920s by some nutritionists who claimed aluminum poisoned food. Many women's magazines took up the issue in the 1920s urging housewives not to prepare acidic foods in aluminum cookware. Various government-sponsored studies of aluminum declared the metal entirely safe for cooking (though the controversy lingered for many decades).

In 1922, twenty-one aluminum-cookware manufacturers, including Monarch, formed the Aluminum Cookware Association to establish standards for the industry, both in the quality and the sale of aluminum products, and to fight against the bad publicity. From 1926 to 1930, the Association spent $100,000 annually to educate the public about aluminum.

Still, the entire industry slumped during the Depression. Many households now could not afford to buy aluminum utensils. The widespread doubts about the quality and safety of aluminum contributed to a negative image that was hard to overcome.

Despite these obstacles, Taylor was convinced of the quality of the Club Aluminum product. He knew there were many satisfied customers using the company's pots and pans.

"The company has high-quality products, excellent personnel with good morale and lots of good will," he said when he took over the company. He also knew the competition was stiff and that Club's cookware was not the only quality product on the market. Club's salesmen suffered from the same poor image all aggressive salesmen had, yet Taylor knew better selling was the key to the renewal of the company. He worked hard to turn the business around, even introducing a new cookware with a hammered finish called Club Hammer-Craft. Even so, by 1932, the worst year of the Depression according to many who lived through it, even the bank had given up. The debt was too burdensome. Karker recommended that Club Aluminum file for bankruptcy. He told Taylor to return full-time to Jewel Tea.

But Taylor surprised everyone when he chose to resign from Jewel Tea and invest everything he had in Club Aluminum. This, he knew, was God's will. Months before he had wrestled with God's purposes for him at this stage in his career.

"I couldn't shake the feeling that God's plan for me was to make the move," he said later. "I was confident I was being directed by God, so I really didn't have any choice." Behind this decision lay a conversation he had with George Perkins (then a YMCA executive, later financier J. Pierpont Morgan's right-hand man) immediately after he returned from France. Taylor asked for Perkins's advice in choosing between youth work through the YMCA or the offer he had from Sinclair Oil in Oklahoma. Perkins spoke plainly: become a success in business and use your extra time to work with youth, so that by the age of forty-five—having become independently wealthy—you can devote yourself fully to young people's projects. Taylor later said, "Mr. Perkins was the vehicle through which I'm certain God presented me with a plan—his particular plan for me. No man could have predicted my life with such accuracy, and surely no one but the Lord could have assured my survival to carry out the plan. From the moment I left Mr. Perkins's office, I knew the course of my life." In almost every way, Taylor's career followed those steps.

Taylor recalled Perkins's suggestion when he considered

the possibility of staying with Club Aluminum. It became apparent that as president he could control the policies of the company in such a way that in later years he could devote more time to youth work. He concluded that God had brought him to the second part of his original plan.

Furthermore, Taylor believed the company should be saved. The employees needed work, and the debts had to be paid. "I prayed for guidance," he admitted. "I added up the rights and wrongs of the case." He determined to wipe out the $400,000 debt. "It was quite apparent that I was the only person convinced that the company could be saved. I was convinced because the Holy Spirit told me so."

Taylor's first steps took courage. He borrowed $6,100 against his Jewel Tea stock. He cut his salary from $33,000 to $6,000; it stayed at that level for the next four years. Gloria did not know until later that Taylor had even put up their own house as collateral.

Taylor then made an important strategic move to give himself freedom to operate. He formed a separate corporation called Club Aluminum Products Company, which had exclusive rights to merchandising Club Aluminum cookware. This new company was strictly a sales organization, but it was one Taylor could control and shape into a strong marketing outfit. The older Club Aluminum company was given forty-nine per cent of the stock in the new firm. Taylor had fifty-one per cent. He was president of both companies until they were merged in 1947.

It was clear that drastic adjustments were needed to restore the fortunes of Club Aluminum. First, Taylor discontinued the home-demonstration method of direct selling, choosing instead to sell cookware in department and grocery stores. It was too costly and had clearly lost some of its popularity among consumers, who were increasingly buying food and household items in stores rather than from traveling salesmen.

Club Aluminum created a mild sensation in late 1933 when the company held a big promotional sale of cookware items at New York's famous Gimbel's department store. It was the first time Club Aluminum had ever sold any products in a store. It was the first time any cookware company had tried this approach. The real excitement, however, was over the fact that the retail price for a Hammer-Craft cookware set was less than half the usual home-demonstration price of $250. Gimbel's sold $90,000 in the first month of the sale. By 1934, Gimbel's was ready for an even larger sales campaign that included full-page newspaper advertising. The results were astounding. Stores in other cities soon became customers.

More innovations followed. In 1935, Taylor began selling cookware through the A & P grocery chain. Club Aluminum salesmen actually cooked roast beef and vegetables on the cookware at a private dinner for each store manager and his employees. The store managers were not only assured a percentage of all sales but were allowed to return unsold goods; the burden of selling rested totally with Club Aluminum personnel. The volume of sales was enormous. Other chains, such as Kroger, Jewel and National, jumped on board with these Household Institutes, as they were called.

The relationship between Club Aluminum and the grocery chains, which by the 1940s were beginning to build supermarkets, was forged during the early years under Taylor's leadership. He explored every avenue to encourage customers to buy his cookware, including the now-familiar special price when purchasing a certain amount of groceries. He sold sets of cookware on almost irresistible terms ($1 down, $1 a week) and offered free trials for housewives that allowed them to take a pan home and try it. He even experimented with direct mail by offering customers free frying pans if they would try the product.

Though Club Aluminum demonstrations and trial offers helped alter aluminum's poor reputation, a 1938 study by Armour Institute's Research Foundation confirmed the quality of the aluminum cookware. "It used considerably less fuel, less supervision by the cook was required, there was less shrinkage in cooking meats and the ware itself was heavy, substantial and had a much longer life," their report concluded. Even though Taylor abhorred extravagant claims, he knew he had a product of which he did not have to be ashamed.

He was not alone in his devotion to the company. Co-workers like Ken Johnston, who was hired in 1937, contributed to the marketing creativity of the company, knowing that they were part of the team and could give their suggestions freely. Not surprisingly, they flourished under the leadership of a true marketing innovator.

The second goal for Club Aluminum was to transform the sales force. Taylor believed that success depended on "a personnel which was of high character and service-minded, considerate of the other fellow." Good products and clever merchandising techniques were not enough. Cookware had to be sold by good people.

To develop such a staff required standards which Taylor thought should be summarized in a code of ethics. A code guided people's thinking. If they thought right, he concluded, they would do right. And if they did what was right, God would bless them and the business.

Taylor mulled over this desire for a guide to right conduct ever since he began with Club Aluminum. He even went to the Chicago Public Library to look for a short measuring stick of ethical behavior suitable for a company like his. In 1932 he came up with his own: the Four-Way Test, a simple code that became one of the most popular ethical guides ever used in American business.

Taylor believed firmly that the Test transformed his company and led to its resurgence. He had some evidence to back up his claim. By 1941 the entire debt of $400,000 carried by the original Club Aluminum was paid off by the profits from the new company, including the interest that accumulated during that period. By the 1940s Club Aluminum was one of the top companies in the sale of cast-aluminum cookware. Even "Club" became a household word that millions of housewives associated with expensive, high-quality cookware which lasted for a lifetime. By 1952 over one million dollars in dividends were paid.

No More Aluminum

Just as the Depression crashed on Taylor's budding career at Jewel, World War II struck a blow to Club Aluminum's remarkable recovery. In March 1941, Taylor and Ken Johnston, by then his assistant, were summoned to Washington, D.C., along with all the other aluminum manufacturers and distributors. There they were informed that all aluminum for domestic production was no longer available. The metal was needed for the war effort.

The effect of this action by the federal government was

immediate. Club Aluminum could sell off its existing stock, but they were effectively put out of the cookware business. The Monarch plant was overhauled to manufacture weapons such as the M-50 magnesium bomb, and many Club Aluminum staff were terminated or took leaves of absence. Taylor scrambled to find other products to sell. He came up with two rather diverse items: flameproof glass coffee makers, manufactured in a Chicago plant, and table games made out of fiberboard and plastic.

During these years, Taylor hired Japanese workers who had been forced to move to the Midwest because their loyalty was suspect. Many of these workers remained with the company after the war ended. Taylor made it clear to them that he did not approve of discrimination.

One year later, Taylor was invited by his former boss, Maurice Karker, to join him on the War Department's Price Adjustment Board as a "dollar-a-year" man. Karker was appointed chairman, and he wanted Taylor to be his vice chairman. Taylor accepted.

The task of the Price Adjustment Board was to review the government contracts of major manufacturing firms to be sure they were not overcharging the government. The board was a self-policing agency with no power to penalize offenders. They could only appeal to a manufacturer's patriotism.

Taylor spent three to four weeks at a time in Washington, D.C., studying the records of thousands of firms with contracts involving more than $100,000 of war business. He observed the usual profiteering by unscrupulous corporations at the expense of the government. In May 1943 Taylor told an audience of manufacturers that his board had uncovered about $2.8 billion in excessive profits. Somewhat tongue-in-cheek, he defined a "fair profit" as "that profit which the contractor would be willing to announce to the men who have left his plant and are serving in the Armed Forces. If you are quite certain those men would believe you had only made a fair profit, then that is a fair profit on war production."

This work brought Taylor into contact with Senator Harry Truman, whose committee was scrutinizing war contracts as well. Like the public at large, Truman was convinced excessive profits were being made by industry in war production. Truman was not altogether pleased with the dollar-a-year men that Franklin Roosevelt's administration recruited, fearing they had vested interests, but he later grudgingly acknowledged their contribution to the war effort. Whether he remembered Taylor, who appeared before him at various hearings, is not known; Taylor himself spoke little about this period of public service in the nation's capital. Yet he set an example of a civic-minded businessman who placed service to his nation above profits.

Taylor served in this role until late 1943 when he resigned over differences about certain "principles and policies" of the Price Adjustment Board. Apparently, Karker resigned because of methods used by the board which he believed were unethical. Taylor joined his friend in protest.

By then, he was glad to return home to his family and his company. He and Johnston had managed affairs through evening and weekend conferences in Chicago and Washington. Incredibly, Club Aluminum never lost money during the war years. Post-war planning began in 1944 and by the following year, as the war ended, the restrictions on the aluminum supply were gradually lifted.

One of the first actions Club's board of directors took after the war was to merge the two Club Aluminum companies. This rather routine business transaction was not without its drama, however. The directors of the original Club Aluminum demanded two-thirds of the stock of the proposed merged company rather than the 50-50 arrangement Taylor proposed. Taylor objected since it was the Club Aluminum Products Company which he started that was responsible for the remarkable growth during the 1930s and the elimination of the debt. An independent evaluation of the two companies' net worth concurred with Taylor's proposal. When it seemed that the entire deal would collapse, Taylor relented and even offered to resign as president. He informed the directors of his Club Aluminum company that he was not interested in fighting. Taylor's college roommate and attorney Lysle Smith, who was also a major stockholder in the company, was mystified by Taylor's response and wanted to go to court over the matter. Taylor refused. "It's the Lord's company," he insisted. "He can protect it."

The other directors persuaded him to remain with the merged company. Within a few years, Taylor bought enough stock from the other investors to regain control. And, as it turned out, the immediate post-war years proved to be the best years in the company's history.

3

The Four-Way Test

Within ten years of taking over Club Aluminum, Herbert J. Taylor made two strategic decisions that transformed his career and the lives of countless men and women. Each of these decisions provides a glimpse into the character of this man, and offers clues to the profound impact he had in both the business and evangelical worlds. The first of these decisions was the creation and promotion of the Four-Way Test; the second was the transfer of a huge share of Club Aluminum stock into the Christian Workers Foundation.

The Four-Way Test, which Taylor developed in 1932, became one of the most popular codes of ethics ever used in American business. It represents a significant contribution to the field of business ethics, an arena in which Christians have much to offer. The Test consists of twenty-four words

phrased in four simple questions:
1. Is it the truth?
2. Is it fair to all concerned?
3. Will it build goodwill and better friendships?
4. Will it be beneficial to all concerned?

Every action, policy or plan was to be subjected to these four criteria. If the answer was yes in all cases, a company or individual could proceed knowing they were on solid moral grounds.

The origin of the Test was actually quite modest. Shortly after taking over at Club Aluminum, Taylor felt the need for a method of measuring the ethical performance of his employees and of his company's relationship to the public. Having determined that high moral standards and a service-minded staff were the key to the rescue of Club Aluminum, Taylor began searching for a practical, easy-to-remember yardstick.

One day Taylor leaned forward at his desk and prayed for an answer to his search. Inspiration came at that precise moment. "I looked up and reached for a white paper card," he wrote in his autobiography. "Then I wrote down the twenty-four words that had come to me." For the remainder of his life, Taylor believed the Test was a gift from God. He refused to take personal credit for its creation. But he promoted it vigorously and applied it diligently.

The first challenge of the Test arose immediately. A tear-sheet for a proposed Club Aluminum advertisement was placed on his desk for his approval. It contained the brash claim "the greatest cooking ware in the world." In Taylor's judgment, it failed the first question of the Four-Way Test. It was not the truth.

Taylor rejected the ad and told his advertising manager to stop using strong superlatives, such as "best" and "finest," and just state the facts. Furthermore, he insisted that no criticisms of competitors' products be included in his company's promotion, since that would hardly build good will and better friendships with other cookware manufacturers.

Such policies were not necessarily suited to a sales-oriented business which relied on media advertising and aggressive selling. One of Taylor's top salesmen told him the Test was not realistic. "Our procedure has always been to sell a dealer as much as we can, even if we load him down with our product," he said. This put pressure on the dealer to promote the product with greater zeal. Taylor argued that this tactic neither built good will nor was it beneficial to the dealer or the customers. He urged the salesmen to be guided by the Test.

Taylor's reasoning was principled but also pragmatic. "Our competitors had good kitchenware, good organization and more money than we had," he said. "I decided the thing we could sell best was integrity." He added, "If we don't let stores overstock our ware and then take back unsold merchandise, they never have an incentive to mark Club Aluminum down. We are enabled thereby to maintain our price levels on a completely voluntary basis."

With the help of his senior managers, Taylor made the Test a visible symbol permeating every nook and cranny of the company. It appeared in the annual reports to stockholders, on the back of salesmen's calling cards and on wall posters, desk plaques and car-window stickers. Employees memorized it, recited it and referred to it in planning and decision-making sessions.

"It became a way of life when I was there," said one executive. "We were very conscious of it. Just the fact that we
enunciated it the way we did had a powerful impact on us
and those with whom we did business."

"Sometimes we were challenged on it," another executive
remembers, "but the top man believed in it and set the example. That's what made it work. And it sunk down to all the
employees. I think it's one reason we had so little turnover.
We were a close team."

When Club Aluminum acquired the Inland Glass Works in
1951, Taylor was forced to deal with unionized workers.
Though he held anti-union sentiments in general, Taylor
was prepared to work with them. His analysis of labor-man-
agement strife was quite simple. It boiled down to selfishness
on both sides.

"Most strikes and lockouts and industrial strife can be
traced directly to selfishness, insincerity, unfair dealings, or
fear or lack of friendship among the men concerned." The
Four-Way Test, as he saw it, met these root problems directly.
He incorporated the Test into the contract which helped
smooth relations between the workers and management.
Taylor also responded to the union demands for improved
working conditions which often arose in contract negotiations. The presence of the Test in the contract made it difficult for the management to ignore their requests. When
Inland Glass was later liquidated, Taylor made sure every
employee had another job before being terminated by the
present company.

The Test undoubtedly cut into profits. On one occasion
during the 1930s the company received a huge order for
50,000 utensils. The cash flow from this sale was needed

badly. But the sales manager discovered the buyer intended to sell the utensils at substantially reduced prices, thus undercutting the regular dealers who were restricted to selling at fixed prices. The decision was painful, but clear. They turned down the order.

Some former Club Aluminum executives and stockholders believed that the Test actually prevented the company from being as profitable as it could have been. Less scrupulous firms would have taken advantage of opportunities that Taylor passed up.

Applying the Test to company practices was not always easy. Indeed, it often complicated matters for certain employees. Taylor's merchandise manager, Don Drumtra, was one who felt the effects of the company's high ethical standards. He handled the customer complaints about the pots and pans, usually over such things as discoloration, the non-durability of the Teflon finish and deficient handles, bushings and knobs. During some years, the volume of letters from dissatisfied customers was enormous.

"I have a feeling we are compounding some of our normal service problems by publicizing what really are our standards of business ethics," Drumtra informed his superiors, "and giving our customers an opportunity to measure us and our product by these rather than the actual performance of our product compared to others of its kind."

In particular, Drumtra was uncomfortable with the practice of including a copy of the Test and a letter from Taylor encouraging customers to write if they were not entirely satisfied with the product. "I am sure they would forget their gripes if we were not so clear, all-inclusive, and specific about who and where to write," he said. "The way we put it on the line, it seems to me too many people expect us to be perfect. We have corrected some of our problems and will make further progress in the future but our product is not perfect and never will be. We are developing a lot of ill will that we really don't deserve."

Taylor personally handled much of the complaint mail, corresponding with literally hundreds of housewives over the years. He was always gracious and generous replacing faulty parts or sending reimbursement. But even his idealism was tempered. At one point, he told his employees they'd do well if they could attain sixty-five per cent application of the Test. Measuring sixty-five per cent of what an employee thinks, says and does was not immediately obvious, but Taylor was compelled to make some room for failure.

Drumtra and others like him did not lack commitment to the Four-Way Test, but they had identified a problem with codes of ethics. While serving a useful purpose in guiding the company policy and employee behavior, high moral standards sooner or later came into conflict with the ultimate goal of every business enterprise: to make a profit. In being fair to the customers, Club Aluminum executives sometimes discovered they weren't being fair to themselves. The cost of resources needed to respond to complaints and the potential loss of sales because of the image these complaints produced made total dedication to the Test difficult to maintain.

To Taylor's credit, he and his coworkers wrestled with the application of morality to the practical, mundane affairs of business. In his analysis of the field of business ethics, Drew University philosopher Donald Jones identifies three central issues: the way we answer the fundamental questions about wealth, work, vocation and leisure; the way a business firm

relates to society, including its customers _____
munity in which it functions; the way man_____
its employees and how the company functio_____
place. Jones suggests that religion and theo_____
thing to offer in each of these areas and _____ and
business leaders should engage in more dialog. Most impor-
tantly, Jones argues, church leaders should show more interest in the practical, day-to-day situations in which business
leaders face ethical dilemmas constantly and where they
need insight to make moral choices. Unfortunately, less than
ten per cent of today's pastors have any experience or knowledge of the challenges businesspeople confront.

There is little evidence that Taylor received much input
from clergymen on business ethics, but he himself attempted
to work out his religious faith through the Four-Way Test. He
occasionally reflected on the philosophical questions of business and profits and—even more often—on the social responsibilities of corporations. Yet his real concern focused
on the personal application of moral principles which he
believed came directly from the Bible.

Several years after developing the Test, Taylor found what
he believed to be biblical justification for it. While preparing
a Sunday-school lesson, he read Jeremiah 9:23-24. The words
leapt off the page.

Thus saith the LORD, Let not the wise man glory in his
wisdom, neither let the mighty man glory in his might, let
not the rich man glory in his riches: But let him that
glorieth glory in this, that he understandeth and knoweth
me, that I am the LORD which exercise lovingkindness,
judgment, and righteousness, in the earth: for in these
things I delight, saith the LORD. (KJV)

There was the Four-Way Test right there," he later told audiences. "Truth, justice and love are the eternal principles on which the Test is based. Every time you apply the Test, you are following these principles." Lovingkindness was the virtue behind the third and fourth questions of the Test. Judgment or justice was the intent of the second question, and righteousness was the idea behind the first.

Taylor took particular delight in quoting the Jeremiah passage, especially to groups of businessmen and professionals. Because the verses were from the Old Testament, he believed they would not offend Catholics, Jews or Protestants. God took pleasure in the values expressed in the Test no matter who practiced them, he believed.

In fact, Taylor asked four persons in the company, one a Christian Scientist, one a Roman Catholic, one an Orthodox Jew and one a Presbyterian, whether anything in the Test conflicted with their religious beliefs. All four said no. He persuaded them to memorize the questions and use them.

For Taylor, the Test was a means of promoting Christian values without using the label "Christian." It appealed to a common belief in God, which crossed most religious boundaries, and the need for acceptance of absolute moral principles essential for any stable society.

Unlike some of his fellow evangelicals, Taylor felt no internal conflict between this ecumenical posture and his own personal adherence to orthodox Christian doctrines. He wanted to see positive results and was quite prepared to be discrete in presenting his particular beliefs. Taylor's personality influenced him as well. He did not like to offend people. He disliked arguments, angry outbursts and broken relationships.

Taylor's use of the Test serves as one model of how religious faith and business interact. They meet in the arena of ethics applied at the level of management and employee relations. Biblical principles are restated in the language of the marketplace. The motivation for following these guidelines is the practical good they bring to individuals and to the whole society. And the results can be measured because right behavior is the final proof.

Taylor's claims on behalf of the Test were grandiose to say the least. He often said, "The Test gets people to think right." If people thought right, it followed that they would act and speak right: good thinking leads to good behavior. Certainly, this maxim has validity.

A person's behavior is affected by ideas, values and beliefs. Even the act of getting someone to think about the consequences of his or her actions can affect behavior. But it is also true that people don't always do what they know they should. Right thinking can be hindered by emotional and psychological needs that cause a person to act to protect himself rather than serve others.

Taylor exerted considerable effort in placing the Test in strategic locations where he thought it could influence the public. Four-Way Test plaques were presented to state governmental officials, members of Congress and Supreme Court judges, often in person by Taylor. Four-Way Test posters were hung on the walls of public high schools; bronze plaques were mounted on major civic buildings. Taylor even tried to get General Motors to place the questions on the instrument panels of Oldsmobiles. In every case, he contended that the Test could improve the behavior of people who read it.

The Four-Way Test Joins Rotary International

Taylor became president of the Chicago Rotary Club in 1938, a prestigious post since the Chicago chapter was the founding group of the entire organization. His contacts with Rotary's board of directors proved to be fruitful. In 1952, he gave them permission to promote the Test, a task welcomed by Rotary members, who were always looking for projects to promote good will, friendship and moral standards. Rotary and the Test were a perfect match.

Rotary members in Daytona Beach, Florida, were responsible for blanketing the city with Four-Way Test stickers, posters and advertisements. They placed windshield stickers in over 15,000 automobiles with the additional question "How does your driving check with the Four-Way Test?" After one year, the juvenile delinquency rate in Daytona Beach dropped twenty per cent and auto accidents declined by a similar rate.

Through the efforts of Rotarians, the South Shore railway line in Chicago installed copies of the Test in all of their passenger cars, stations and offices. After several years, company executives reported better relations between management and unions.

A special Rotary project in Kenosha, Wisconsin, placed Test posters and plaques throughout the city's high schools, the first of many U.S. high schools to engage in this form of values education. In Kenosha, the Test proved to be a standard to which both teachers and students held each other accountable. It was also a useful discussion topic and a familiar theme of commencement addresses.

Rotary International became so infatuated with the Test that they encouraged every club to establish a Four-Way Test committee for the purpose of promoting and encouraging its use. Many clubs offered scholarships to high-school students who often delivered speeches on some aspect of the Test. Others looked for ways to display the Test in public places.

Rotary also distributed the Test to 169 countries in which their clubs were located. Japanese Rotarians were especially active in making the Test prominent in their schools and at railroad stations.

It was little wonder that Taylor was chosen for the one-year term of president of Rotary International during its fiftieth anniversary celebrated in 1954-55. That same year he and Gloria traveled around the globe addressing clubs on the virtues of the Test. His speeches included accounts of the Test's results and of the need for moral standards.

The Test and the Decline of Ethics

Businessmen have always been sensitive to the moral climate, realizing that a certain level of honesty and good will is essential for business to be transacted. Taylor feared the decline of ethics and widespread chaos more than anything else. Even Communism, the ogre of the post-war era, was a moral threat to him, not merely a political one. He worried about juvenile delinquency, alcoholism, racial strife, disregard for traffic laws and dishonesty in business. In Chicago, political corruption was almost institutionalized. The notorious mayor of Chicago, William "Big Bill" Thompson, had made a farce of city government, condoning widespread disregard for Prohibition, gang warfare in the streets, bribery of police, and misuse of city workers and schoolteachers for political tasks. His successor, Edward Kelly, was a bit more discrete, but the political machine he built in the 30s and 40s hardly operated according to strict ethical standards. All of these were problems at which the Test was aimed.

But the Test was not merely a formula. There were assumptions that went along with it. A belief in God and his ultimate authority together with the stewardship for the earth and all it contains were implied. So was the need for prayer and Bible reading. Only through religious renewal would there be the strengthening of moral and ethical standards.

In an interesting conversation in 1960 with a Chicago corporate executive on the subject of ethics and business, Taylor bluntly argued that divine guidance and spiritual faith were absolute prerequisites for ethical standards to be raised. The executive disagreed, observing that religious people were too prone to be sectarian, to push their particular doctrines, to use religion to justify their own moral failures.

In the end, for Taylor, the Test was a way of pointing people to God and to a responsible, satisfying way of life. For all people are accountable to God for what they have been given, Taylor often said in his speeches. Everything you possess is given to you as a trust, and someday you will give an account of yourself. The Four-Way Test is a helpful way to put your resources to the best use. God will be pleased with you.

4

Foundations: Five Youth Organizations

Bᵧ the late 1930s, Herbert Taylor sensed that another stage in God's plan for his life was about to begin. He had reached the age at which George Perkins had predicted he would be spending as much time on youth work as he did in business. Many experiences in his career were already pointing in that direction. Club Aluminum was back on its feet and growing rapidly. The company had nearly paid off its remaining debts. The lessening of this pressure gave him more time to devote to other concerns.

But more significantly, Taylor was developing a passion for youth evangelism. During the entire 1930s, both Taylors were active in a storefront mission church on the near-north side of Chicago, a destitute section of the city. The mission operated a bread line as well as a Sunday school and evangelistic services. Gloria sang regularly at these services, while Taylor taught and administered the mission.

Taylor's concern for the children and families he encountered at the mission led him to survey the entire neighborhood. Approaching the matter like a business problem, he discovered that at least fifty per cent of the children had no connection with any church or Sunday school, nor was there much interest among their families in attending church. Taylor concluded that some other means was necessary to reach these children; the church was unable to do the job. Nondenominational organizations had to be created to evangelize children and teen-agers, who could then enter the churches as converts. The idea of working outside the established church was not new, but it took a courageous layman to move ahead on his own.

In 1940, after praying with Gloria for a number of months, Taylor took the step. He set up the Christian Worker's Foundation, a nonprofit foundation to launch and support organizations committed to evangelizing youth, and he gave twenty-five per cent of the Club Aluminum stock to the foundation. The trustees of the foundation, besides himself, were Gloria and his college roommate, Lysle Smith, who was now his attorney. The dividends from the stock were distributed to the organizations and projects which fulfilled their agendas. Within a year, Taylor hired a young journalist from Northwestern University, Robert Walker, to handle the administrative duties for the foundation and assist him in launching national youth organizations. Walker, a fellow Methodist who had attended Wheaton College in order to play football and was later converted to the evangelical cause, soon found himself editing a Christian magazine for college students, serving on several boards and coordinating the work of these same agencies.

Taylor's goal was to "pioneer and finance the nondenominational organizations we felt would do the best job of reaching young people." In particular, he wanted to establish national agencies for youth at every age level from preschoolers to collegians. The foundation's assistance was to be more than monetary. Said Taylor, "We contributed the know-how to assume practical success to organizations guided by men with strong ideals and convictions, who also needed sound business judgment to guarantee the furtherance of their goals. It seems they needed us, and we needed them." To make this contribution, Taylor required that either he or Walker become members of an organization's board of directors if the foundation was to provide regular funding. As a result, Taylor served on forty-five boards and committees during his life.

InterVarsity Christian Fellowship

The first organization to receive foundation money was InterVarsity Christian Fellowship, a British campus ministry that had migrated to Canada in 1927. Though several Inter-Varsity chapters had formed on American university campuses, the U.S. organization was not established until Taylor persuaded the Canadian board to move its director, Stacey Woods, to Chicago where he would work out of the foundation offices with an annual budget of $10,000. Woods moved to Chicago in 1941 and traveled extensively, establishing chapters on all the major campuses (over 500 by 1950), overseeing a growing staff of full-time campus evangelists and conducting summer training programs for Christian college students on a 3,000-acre tract of land in northern Michigan donated by Taylor. Walker, meanwhile, produced the new InterVarsity publication *His*, which Taylor and Woods launched. In 1948, Taylor brought the student missionary convention to the University of Illinois campus at Urbana, where 1,200 students met over the Christmas vacation to be inspired by missionary speakers.

Woods admired Taylor immensely because "he was a man who did more to introduce Christian principles, particularly on the basis of the Sermon on the Mount, into his business practice than any man I have known." As chairman of the IVCF board, Taylor worked intimately with Woods, in fact, to such a degree that insiders complained, "H. J. Taylor and Stacey Woods rigged everything to suit themselves."

Fireball Evangelism
At the same time that Taylor was building the InterVarsity ministry, he was attempting to harness the energy of a fireball youth evangelist in Texas named Jim Rayburn, who was drawing hordes of teen-agers to his after-school clubs and summer tent meetings. In 1940, Rayburn and his fellow seminarians from the conservative Dallas Theological Seminary dubbed their new organization Young Life Campaign.

Taylor was immediately attracted to Rayburn's approach and agreed to underwrite his salary. "Essentially, his whole theory was to go out to unchurched, uninterested young people and attract them to Christ," Taylor recalled, "rather than drive them to Christ. Jim presented the gospel without long sermons. He did it with a fire and enthusiasm that appealed to young people, who might never, in a million years, step inside a church on their own. Jim's 'strange' way of reaching these youngsters of high-school age was just what we needed."

Taylor's only stipulation was that Rayburn extend his work across the country. "You'll have to go national, Rayburn, or I'll not give you another dime." Rayburn was most obliging; by 1967, Young Life clubs reached over 50,000 teen-agers nationwide, and four ranches owned by the organization attracted 10,000 young people each summer.

Committed to Youth

Three other organizations received Taylor's special attention: Child Evangelism Fellowship, Pioneer Girls and Christian Service Brigade. They were organizations dedicated to evangelizing children and young teens who were outside the Protestant church. Each was led by individuals with intense zeal but little organizational savvy. Each was in desperate need of financial support.

Child Evangelism Fellowship was organized after Taylor met a California evangelist, J. Irvin Overholtzer, who had started Good News Clubs for young children. Overholtzer relied on mothers to teach elementary schoolchildren in their homes after school using flannelgraphs to tell Bible stories. Taylor was impressed with the success of this method and persuaded Overholtzer to head a national organization.

Child Evangelism grew steadily especially after World War II. By the mid-60s, there were over 900,000 children attending 10,000 Good News Clubs. In addition, the organization had sent over 150 missionaries to do a similar type of evangelistic work in other countries.

Pioneer Girls was the product of several Wheaton College students whose zeal for weekday girls' clubs continued after their graduation in 1942. Carol Erickson and Louise Troup had organized several clubs in the western suburbs of Chicago while they were students and had also developed curriculum material with an early-American theme. They continued to promote the concept of "putting Christ into every phase of a girl's life" by writing more literature and staying in touch with other girls-club leaders.

Erickson and Troup contacted Taylor in 1943 after he helped Wheaton College alumnus Joseph Coughlin establish his boys' club organization called Christian Service Brigade. Pioneer Girls had been, in effect, a subsidiary of Coughlin's operation; Erickson and Troup wanted their own separate organization. Taylor agreed and began to subsidize them through his foundation. He insisted on incorporation with a constitution and board of directors, on which he and Gloria both served. Rebecca Price, a Wheaton College professor, was asked to chair the board. She functioned in that role for the next twenty-seven years and became a close friend of Taylor's.

The first office of Pioneer Girls was located at the same location as the Christian Worker's Foundation, then on the thirty-first floor of Chicago's Civic Opera building. A Detroit club leader, Lois Thiessen, took over the organization in 1944 after Erickson and Troup decided to pursue graduate studies.

Taylor kept in regular contact with the Pioneer Girls leadership during the following decades. The organization grew constantly, reaching almost 2500 churches with some 23,000 registered club leaders and 90,000 girls by the mid-70s. It also established seventeen camps across the country.

Christian Service Brigade was launched in a similar way.

Throughout his adult life, Taylor had done volunteer work with boys and even became a member of the National Committee on Work with Boys where he interacted with Boy Scout and YMCA officials. The epidemic of juvenile delinquency, as it was perceived in the 1940s with the help of J. Edgar Hoover's FBI propaganda machine, worried Taylor. In his view, it was "a matter of religious training—of guiding young people toward the eternal values of honesty, faith and high principles."

We knew we could strike out at the heart of the major problem facing the country—the lack of spiritual and ethical training for millions of young people. Some of the religious powers took a rather narrow view of the Christian Worker's Foundation. In those days, they didn't know who we were and they were suspicious of our desire to help make these organizations nondenominational. But we soon demonstrated the integrity of our efforts and God greatly blessed these projects in His service. Our only concern was the spiritual welfare of young people, and this objective was clearly in evidence from the beginning.

Since most juvenile delinquents were boys, Taylor was especially fond of the young collegians who pioneered the Brigade organization.

Taylor's first contact with Christian Service Brigade came in 1940 when he decided to help Coughlin, then a Wheaton College student, with the financial burdens of his new boys' organization. Taylor assigned his associate, Walker, to provide managerial leadership for the cluster of Brigade units in the Chicago area. The Christian Worker's Foundation also provided Coughlin with an office and the use of Taylor's Prentiss Bay property in northern Michigan for the third summer of Camp Kaskitowa, a primitive adventure camp for teen-age boys led by Coughlin.

In 1943, Taylor assumed an even stronger leadership role by becoming chairman of the board of directors, making Walker the general secretary. The foundation also began funding the Brigade organization at $400 per month (by the end of the year this was reduced to $225). Always concerned about the national picture, Taylor cultivated relationships with evangelical boys' organizations in Detroit and New England, eventually bringing about a merger of the three groups. Finally, through Walker's initiative, Taylor brought Kenneth Hansen, a young Chicago seminarian, to the Brigade staff as the first full-time general secretary.

For the next five years, Taylor continued to be a dominant presence on the CSB board. He saw great potential for the Brigade movement and its sister organization, Pioneer Girls. Perhaps his fond memories of boyhood days in Michigan's Upper Peninsula encouraged him to support Coughlin's ambitious camp programs and the elaborate ritual which the imaginative collegian injected into the boys' club program.

Taylor also pushed Hansen to establish policies for managing and raising funds. For example, he wanted all new staff members to be fully deputized before they began their work. He pressed Hansen and Coughlin to charge an annual registration fee of 25 cents (always the diplomat, Taylor listened patiently to their protests for several years until they relented). Constantly he suggested ways to improve fund-raising appeals, and he personally made contacts with potential donors.

As a creator of youth organizations, Taylor was always alert to their growth and their cooperation with each other, including merging their operations. On several occasions, he advocated bringing together the Brigade and Pioneer Girls organizations to maximize efficiency in servicing churches. The closest he ever got to this goal was two short-lived appointments of executive secretaries who supervised both organizations simultaneously.

When Taylor stepped down as board chairman in 1948, the Brigade organization was on its feet, though wobbly at times. Nearly 300 churches were involving over 5,000 boys in the Brigade program in twenty-four states. Nine Brigade camps were in operation, and a full range of boys' and leaders' literature was available. New staff members had expanded the work and given the Brigade staff a new look: Werner Graendorf replaced Ken Hansen, and Joe Coughlin had taken a leave of absence to do missionary work in Costa Rica. Taylor continued to serve on the board's candidate committee, taking the opportunity to screen new staff prospects.

Beyond these five youth organizations that Taylor nurtured into self-sufficiency were a host of agencies, programs and individuals who obtained his financial support and, in many cases, his personal interest. Over 200 organizations were recipients of gifts from the Christian Worker's Foundation. They included evangelistic organizations, Bible colleges, political organizations (almost always Republican) and study centers (such as the American Institute of Holy Land Studies). Though he was in principle opposed to unions, he was not above making contributions to the welfare funds of his employees' unions.

Invariably, Taylor gradually reduced his contributions to an agency over a period of years in order to stimulate them to develop a broader base of support. "We cut new trails, tried new ideas, experimented with new systems and methods," Taylor said. "Everything the Christian Worker's Foundation was connected with during all these years can appropriately be called pioneering."

Foundation funds not only helped to convert these humble enterprises into viable, growth-oriented organizations, but they created a network of independent evangelical agencies geared to impact American culture in ways which Protestant churches had been unable to do for almost a century. Taylor's initial interest in youth eventually grew to a commitment to enhancing the status of the once-ridiculed evangelicals and mobilizing them to regain a position of influence.

5

Club Aluminum Booms

The decade following World War II boomed for American business. Instead of a recession, the economy erupted as consumers eagerly purchased automobiles, homes, household appliances and recreational equipment, things denied them during the war.

For Club Aluminum the period from 1947 to 1955 was marked by healthy profits and strong marketing success. Net sales peaked in 1948 at over $13 million, placing the firm among the top aluminum cookware distributors in the nation. The $1.65-per-share dividend that year was one of the best the company had ever managed. The aluminum-wares industry as a whole was growing by leaps and bounds rapidly.

The Korean War dampened the excitement somewhat as aluminum supplies were once again curtailed. It wasn't until

1959 that the volume of sales regained the level of the late 40s. Nevertheless, these were years of solid growth for the company. New product lines were introduced, such as porcelain-enameled aluminum ware. Several small manufacturing companies, including a knife company, were purchased. National advertising through *Life* and *Better Homes and Gardens* magazines reaffirmed the company's public image as a high-quality cookware line. Internally, a profit-sharing plan for employees was instituted which helped to encourage innovation and extra effort.

The company environment encouraged employees to suggest ideas and test them in the marketplace. "We had a lot of fun in those days," recalled one executive. "We'd try almost anything. Sometimes, it was like a circus." Obviously, Taylor encouraged this kind of spirit because it was so characteristic of how he operated. He enjoyed the challenge of merchandising and, like a person drilling for oil, he was always looking for success.

Two new faces joined the management team during these years: Taylor's son-in-law, Allen Mathis, and Charlie Cecil, a close friend of Mathis. Both Mathis and Cecil graduated from the Harvard Business School after the war. Cecil had no plans to enter a sales firm but was charmed by Taylor. He began working at Club Aluminum in 1947. Mathis first went to Continental Illinois Bank in Chicago where he stayed until 1952, becoming a second vice president. He then became a vice president at Club the same year Taylor took the position of chairman of the board and Ken Johnston took over as president.

Ken Johnston had been Taylor's faithful assistant since 1937, serving as a reliable "inside man" while Taylor provided the more public profile. The two worked well together. Both had acquired their management skills through years of experience and dogged determination. Mathis and Cecil, on the other hand, came with business-school perspectives and differing ideas on management and marketing which often produced lively tensions within the company. Old and new schools of management theory clashed. Taylor was tolerant, if not appreciative, of the ferment.

Taylor's attentions had gradually shifted and he was spending far less time in his office dealing with the company's business. He had been loosening his grip on the company's day-to-day operations all through the 1940s. The Christian Worker's Foundation was consuming a day per week as he nursed the various struggling organizations he had launched.

In addition, Rotary commitments continued to demand more time. In 1946, he became a vice president of the international organization after having been a district governor and director. Every step up the ranks of Rotary meant more speaking engagements, more conferences and more travel. Then, in 1947, a serious illness incapacitated him for many months. It was a blow which had several positive consequences.

Herbert, Gloria and daughter Beverly endured the same sickness—undulant fever—together. This rare illness was a low-grade infection that weakened resistance to other diseases. Their doctors were stumped in their search for a cure (although they would later trace the disease to unpasteurized milk purchased by the Taylors in Oklahoma almost twenty-five years before). Herbert did not think he would survive.

The turning point came when Taylor's friend Charles

Fuller came to visit and discuss his plans to start a theological seminary. Fuller wanted Taylor's financial and personal help and prayed to God for deliverance from the illness. The prayer was answered and Taylor recovered, as did his wife and daughter.

Taylor's friendship with Fuller deepened in the following years. He helped the evangelist begin a conservative evangelical seminary in Pasadena, California, and was one of the seminary's first trustees. The first meeting of the Fuller trustees was held in Taylor's office in Chicago. The foundation donated $1,000 a year to the seminary plus numerous scholarships for students. Taylor remained a trustee for the rest of his life. He took particular delight in the many graduates who joined the ranks of the youth organizations he had created.

Taylor and the Sermon on the Mount
While bedridden in his house, Taylor began memorizing the Sermon on the Mount. After contemplating Jesus' words in John 14:21, "He that hath my commandments, and keepeth them, he it is that loveth me," he decided to absorb Jesus' directions in Matthew 5—7 into his thinking and actions.

From 1947 to the end of his life, Taylor recited the Sermon on the Mount daily, along with twenty other chapters, including John 14—17, Isaiah 53 and 55, and Romans 8 and 12. It was a remarkable accomplishment for a man in his mid-50s. It so impressed Billy Graham, then a young, not-so-famous evangelist, that he often referred to Taylor's habit in his sermons. Graham's admiration of Taylor was later instrumental in getting Graham to conduct two crusades in Chicago.

The effect of Christ's great sermon on Taylor's ethics was considerable. "In those beautiful words," he said, "is the formula for peace, for brotherhood, and for all the fine things for which men have yearned since the dawn of creation." In the sermon are also specific guidelines for loving one's enemies, and settling differences with others. Indeed, the entire sermon probes the inner motivations for our actions and challenges the pretenses of religious leaders. It's a call for genuine living and for sincere dependence on God.

Those who knew Taylor well were impressed primarily by his character. They spoke of his warmth and friendliness, his uncanny ability to persuade people and achieve consensus, his absolute integrity and a personality that was charming and profoundly attractive. The casual observer can only assume that his daily exposure to the Sermon on the Mount had produced these results.

However, Taylor was not without his enemies. Two of them were major stockholders in Club Aluminum. Martin Schultes was a New York investor who owned sizable stock in the original Club Aluminum Utensil Company. When the two Club companies were merged in 1946, Schultes was convinced that Taylor maneuvered the negotiations to his own advantage.

He was irritated with the large amount of stock owned by Taylor's foundation. Furthermore, he resented the profit-sharing plan Taylor introduced because it included all employees. Schultes wanted to limit the plan to long-term employees. The office and warehouse workers were of no concern to him.

A more vocal critic of Taylor was Carl Hellberg, a long-time friend and a former colleague from Jewel Tea. Hellberg went into business for himself but kept Club Aluminum stock as part of his investment portfolio. After the war, he became increasingly dissatisfied with the dividends he was receiving from Club. Convinced that Club Aluminum should be more profitable, and angry that some profits were being returned to employees rather than stockholders, Hellberg chastised Taylor constantly. He attacked Taylor for not working full-time at Club Aluminum. He wanted Taylor to be more competitive, more bothered by the higher value of other cookware manufacturers' stock, more willing to seek mergers with other companies to maximize earnings.

"There is only one medium of appraisal which will reflect what the public as a whole thinks about any company," Hellberg wrote in a caustic letter to Taylor. "Namely, the price that they are willing to pay for that company's stock." Character and good reputation were fine, he said, but in the final analysis they weren't as important as profitability.

The friendship between the two men became very strained. Even still, Taylor loaned his "thorn in the flesh" an amount of $5,000 when Hellberg found himself in need. Taylor told his colleagues he was "heaping coals" on Hellberg's head, a reference to Romans 12:20. His patience was legendary. Hellberg's ranting proved this quality beyond a doubt. In the end, both Schultes and Hellberg sold their stock in Club Aluminum and, in disgust, washed their hands of a company that refused to do what they felt should be done to increase profits.

"Club Time"

Another source of conflict between Taylor and Hellberg was Club Aluminum's foray into religious broadcasting. From

1946 to 1954, Club Aluminum sponsored a weekly, then monthly, radio broadcast, "Club Time," on the ABC network. The program consisted of hymns and Scripture reading and only a brief mention of any Club Aluminum product. It was a venture that Taylor enjoyed greatly and gave up reluctantly. Hellberg thought it was a waste of money.

Taylor had two reasons for launching such a radio program. First, he wanted to advertise but in a way that honored God and fulfilled the Four-Way Test. At the same time advertising agencies, like Leo Burnett in Chicago, told Taylor of the huge radio audiences available. In 1946, eighty-five per cent of American families owned at least one radio. The average family listened to their radio almost four hours per day. Furthermore, the radio medium was ideally suited for advertising—a human voice could be extremely persuasive.

Taylor had already begun advertising Club's products in *Life* and several national women's magazines. He had discovered through a market survey in 1946 that only ten per cent of the interviewed women were familiar with the Club name. It was clear that the pre-war reputation had worn off. The huge population of post-war brides simply did not recognize the Club Aluminum name. To solve this problem, Club Aluminum had to resort to high-profile national advertising in order to re-establish its name in the public mind. The cost of this type of advertising was very high, but in the late 1940s it paid rich dividends for Club Aluminum. Millions of customers became familiar with the splashy, four-color, full-page advertisements appearing in major magazines with such slogans as "It looks like silver, cooks like magic and lasts a lifetime."

Secondly, Taylor was attracted to radio because of the opportunities to inspire and influence the public. He knew the loyalty of audiences to preachers like Charles Fuller, not to mention the more famous performers like Jack Benny, Fibber McGee, Walter Winchell, Fred Allen and Bob Hope. Corporations like General Mills, DuPont and Kraft had discovered the commercial potential of radio entertainment.

He determined to broadcast hymns because that would "bring a blessing" to the listeners. He personally had a deep appreciation for the great hymns of the church. Hymns were a means of communicating the gospel and the values of the Christian faith. They taught even as they soothed the soul. Hymns were also what many people wanted to hear on the radio, according to several listener polls. Religious programming was a popular dimension of radio along with comedy, drama, music and news.

Taylor's unique contribution was the novel idea of presenting the favorite hymns of famous people. To obtain this information Taylor sent Walker, who worked for the foundation but also belonged to Club's board of directors, to interview well-known personalities. Telephone or letter contact was not adequate. Taylor insisted on a face-to-face contact. Walker ended up in the offices of such notables as Eddie Rickenbacker, General Omar Bradley, Lowell Thomas, J. Edgar Hoover, Frances Perkins and Babe Ruth, always with the same simple request.

The other brilliant move was the recruitment of soloist George Beverly Shea to sing the hymns along with an eleven-voice choir. Shea was working at Moody Bible Institute in Chicago at the time, and few people had heard his rich baritone voice. The "Club Time" broadcast established his reputation and paved the way for Shea to join Billy Graham's evangelistic team in the 1950s. Organist Don Hustad also got his beginnings on "Club Time" and eventually joined Graham and Shea.

The format of "Club Time" was very simple. Walker wrote the scripts for the narrator who introduced the hymns and the Scripture readings (almost always from Psalms). Both of Taylor's daughters handled the Bible-reading chores. Beverly had embarked on a free-lance professional career as a broadcasting actress; she did commercials and acted in the radio soap operas "Road of Life," "Backstage Wife" and "Woman in White" (later, she had a part in an early television program called "Welcome to the Walkers"). For her, the weekly "Club Time" program was always her most enjoyable radio experience. Her sister, Ramona, was selected to replace her several years later when Beverly moved to Boston.

"Club Time" was an immense success. Its listener ratings were excellent. A Chicago Hooper Rating in 1947 placed them at 3.4 compared to the Metropolitan Opera at 4.2, "Lutheran Hour" at 2.8 and Charles Fuller at 1.8. These ratings translated into a weekly audience of over two million. The program was heard on almost seventy ABC-affiliated stations. Nielsen in 1949 said that "Club Time" was getting two to three per cent of the audience, compared to nine per cent for heavyweight Arthur Godfrey. Network executives were genuinely impressed at the success of "Club Time," especially since it was initially broadcast on Saturday morning and featured no celebrities.

Huge volumes of letters were received at Club Aluminum, almost all appreciative of the hymns and Shea's renditions of them. Close to a third of this mail included requests for information about, or actual orders for, aluminum cookware.

The broadcast itself avoided direct-sales pitches, but the association between the hymns and Club Aluminum products was almost always favorable. Said Taylor, "We have successfully steered away from self-righteousness, preaching, sectarianism and commercialism." Like the Four-Way Test, "Club Time" was a soft-sell approach that served a wider public with a muted Christian message. It was Taylor's way of doing business.

But the costs of sponsoring a radio program were climbing, and, after the Korean War started, Club's profits declined. The broadcast was reduced from thirty minutes to fifteen, then from weekly to monthly, to cut costs. Eventually, it was dropped altogether. Shea recalled Taylor's "sweetness of spirit" when he informed the "Club Time" personnel that the end had come. "He explained it so carefully," Shea said, "in the spirit of Christ. It was so different than the way most agencies treated us."

There was no cost-benefit analysis after "Club Time" folded. Company executives acknowledged the enormous good will generated by the program but knew it was hard to measure its profitability. No other cookware manufacturer was investing as much in radio as Club was. Taylor continued as long as he could with a project that reflected the service ideal of the Four-Way Test far more than the desire to sell cookware.

Diversifying Club Aluminum

Selling was still Taylor's preoccupation when his attention focused on the business. Increasingly, he and his executives realized that cast-aluminum cookware was a limited market in which to sell. The durability of the pots and pans was both a strength and a weakness. A sale of an entire set was often a one-time sale. The logical marketing response was to sell the same customer some other products as well. In other words, Club Aluminum needed to find more ways to serve the same people.

The first move in this diversification strategy occurred in 1951 when Club Aluminum purchased Inland Glass Works of Chicago, the same firm that manufactured coffee makers during the war. Inland was also producing glass carafes and globes for electrical lighting.

In 1955, Club Aluminum acquired the Supermarket Service Division, a North Carolina company which handled houseware rack sales in supermarkets. About 1,000 stores, mostly in the eastern half of the country, participated in the program at some time. This approach was profitable in its best years but also a headache to supervise. Store managers were an independent breed and rarely followed the guidelines provided by Taylor or his salesmen.

Cookware manufacturing was never a static business. Technological breakthroughs occurred constantly. After the war, aluminum cookware with a colored porcelain-exterior finish was developed. This innovation enabled companies, like Club, to sell a more attractive pot or pan. The Club Holiday line using the porcelain finish was introduced in 1955. Another technique of polishing the aluminum, called Velvaglaze, was begun in 1948 as an alternative to the hammered finish of the more traditional pot or pan.

At the same time, stainless steel made its appearance in the marketplace. It had some distinct advantages over aluminum and iron cookwares: lighter weight; shining, attractive appearance; and a finish that did not chip, crack or discolor.

Stainless steel could not claim to be waterless, however; food could stick or burn on its surface. Taylor chose to stay with cast aluminum, but the competition had become much stiffer, and he was no longer able to work as hard, or devote the time needed, to meet the challenge. As a result, the company struggled.

The turning point came in 1954 when Taylor was notified that he had been chosen by Rotary International's board of directors to be its president for the Golden Anniversary year. Though a distinct honor, it was not without its cost: Taylor was expected to take a leave of absence for a year from his business duties and travel around the world on behalf of Rotary.

In that year, Taylor and Gloria made a 25,000-mile trip visiting thirty-eight countries and over 600 Rotary Clubs. It was treated like a royal tour, complete with receptions at government and embassy locations, audiences with heads of state, balls and banquets, visits to Rotary-sponsored projects and endless speeches. The governments of nine countries, including Egypt, France, Italy and Syria, decorated Taylor when he and Gloria visited those nations. The world travels were supplemented by visits to several hundred Rotary gatherings across the United States.

The extravaganza culminated with an international convention in Chicago in June 1955, where Taylor presided over a gathering of 15,000 Rotarians and their families. He even made the cover of *Newsweek* magazine that year, which included a brief biographical sketch and a portrait of Rotary as "a brand of internationalism" which had "broken through the barriers of race, religion and language as government and church have seldom been able to do."

It was a well-deserved year of celebration for a hard-working man, but it marked the end of Herbert Taylor's productive years in the cookware business.

6

Moving On: Selling Club Aluminum

By most standard definitions, Herbert Taylor was an entrepreneur. He saw new ways of doing things and was prepared to take risks to accomplish his goals. Though his knowledge of cookware-manufacturing technology was not extensive, he was a problem-solver and an innovator. He kept looking for better designs and more effective ways to merchandise. Problems, whether in manufacturing or distribution, rarely demoralized him; most often, they intensified his desire to meet a need. Obstacles energized him.

Entrepreneurs excel at getting a business started and, often against great odds, making it successful. They are not always effective in managing companies after they have achieved success. Maintaining the status quo runs against their grain. In fact, they are often counterproductive when a business falters or becomes stuck in a rut. Entrepreneurs want to try the old methods that worked years before, but the conditions that once produced success have changed. They can't resurrect the business they began.

Companies launched by entrepreneurs are by no means doomed to decline. They can be renewed, even transformed. They can change their entire product line, their methods of distribution or the manner in which they service their customers. They can change their clientele or merge with other companies. Organizational renewal, however, often comes from "intrapreneurs," those people whose creativity and imagination are aimed at remodeling the existing structures of a company. Rather than building a new house, they make an old house like new.

In the case of Club Aluminum, Taylor was clearly the entrepreneurial force responsible for the company's success in the Depression and early post-war years. By force of personality, hard work and genuine dependence on God, he forged a strong company with high-quality products. Nevertheless, the company's growth leveled off in the 1950s, and Taylor was unable to engineer any significant expansion of the business.

His personal circumstances were partly the reason. In 1955, when he completed his triumphant year as Rotary's president, he was sixty-two years old. Poor health had plagued him occasionally since the bout with undulant fever in 1947. His life plan called for less time with the company and more time with the Christian Worker's Foundation's projects. Normally, he spent only three days a week at the Club Aluminum office, which in 1957 was moved from downtown Chicago to the suburb of LaGrange Park. Extensive travel reduced even this level of commitment to the business.

Taylor had, in effect, become a traveling lay evangelist, and Club Aluminum was his platform. His message was a blend of the Four-Way Test, the virtues of prayer and Bible memorization, the need in American society for higher moral standards, and folksy advice, especially to teen-agers, on being successful in life. He told his life story on television talk shows, in *Guideposts* magazine, at high-school assemblies and at countless Rotary luncheons. Both he and Club Aluminum became symbols in the business world and in the evangelical community, symbols that inspired thousands of people.

Surveying Club Aluminum

Taylor's absence from the office was not the major problem. Because he controlled fifty-one per cent of the company's stock, he still determined the direction of the company. His choice of company officers prevailed, and his image of the company's purpose and position in the marketplace remained a persistent influence. Not that any rebellion or power struggle ever occurred; Taylor was too well liked by everyone in the firm. Admiration of him kept executives and salesmen working hard to improve the quality of the cookware and find new markets in which to sell it.

Even so, the lack of steady growth was frustrating, and the pressure to improve the company's performance through "reorganization" of the business built up on several occasions. The impetus for change usually came from Allen Mathis and Charlie Cecil, who pressed for evaluations by outside management consultants.

In 1958, the Peat, Marwick, Mitchell firm conducted an

extensive study of Club Aluminum's management systems and its supermarket-merchandising operation. They interviewed all the personnel with managerial responsibilities, asking them to identify the strengths and weaknesses of the company. Though not scientifically accurate, the results of this informal assessment were quite revealing.

The men who sold Club products (there were few, if any, women in leadership roles at Club during these years) were loyal, committed individuals. They clearly felt a sense of ownership in the business, primarily because they had been treated with respect. The dedication of Taylor and his top management to developing and supporting employees was genuinely appreciated, even when incompetence was tolerated "in an unusually thoughtful and kind fashion," as one manager put it. In addition, they were optimistic about the future, believing that the Club Aluminum name carried a positive reputation with the buying public.

These same managers were able to put their fingers on some serious problems, however. They acknowledged the company's primary strength—its expertise and success in sales promotion—but worried that the margins on these sales were too narrow and the costs of running promotions too high. They recommended more attention be paid to non-promotional sales which could be more steady and profitable.

But this suggestion encountered other problems. Maintaining inventories and reliable distribution of cookware, dinnerware and glassware was a demanding task requiring tight controls, good communication and careful supervision by office and branch managers. Club's track record in this area was not very good.

The fact that Club did not control manufacturing was another obstacle. The Monarch plant in Cleveland did all the product development and manufacturing. Though they were an innovative company that made several breakthroughs with cast aluminum, the Monarch executives were not always able or willing to respond to the requests of Club's sales force.

At one time in the late 1940s, Club (with Taylor) owned forty per cent of Monarch's stock and entered negotiations with Monarch's president, Raymond Deutsch, to merge the two companies. But Deutsch passed away and his successor, Eddie Bloomberg, proved to be less accommodating. The potential deal collapsed. Though Taylor was not perturbed by the struggle between the two companies, his executives felt that Club had assumed all the risks, by ordering huge quantities of cookware from Monarch, and lacked the necessary control over the quality of the finished product.

Club Aluminum's men were irritated that a simple problem like a durable pot handle could not be solved to the satisfaction of customers. One irate customer wrote Taylor after searching in vain for a replacement handle for her thirty-year-old Club Aluminum pot: "Mr. Taylor, what are you going to do about my pot handle? I am dumping my problem square in your lap. That is where it belongs. I have my own [problems] to cope with and if you think it is easy, then I suggest you try running a home!" Taylor sent her a gracious letter, two plastic handles and a complimentary frying pan. The discoloration and staining of the aluminum interior was also an embarrassment and a matter of constant concern within the company.

Inland Glass, now a subsidiary, was losing ground as well.

The carafes it manufactured were still handblown, while the competitors were operating with automatic blowing equipment.

All these difficulties pointed to a deeper problem facing Club's management team, a problem fixated on a certain type of product and a certain way of selling it. "Our thinking is principally pot and pan," one manager told the consultants. What was needed was to become an integrated sales and manufacturing company which did not rely so heavily on high-powered sales campaigns, the method Taylor had used with such success decades earlier. Furthermore, some of the managers wanted the company to produce and sell ceramic and stainless-steel cookware, which Corning and Revere-Ware were marketing effectively.

Expansion required a long-range plan for product development and more training for branch managers. Authority and responsibility needed to be delegated to these individuals so they could establish strong, regional sales programs and remove employees who were not performing well.

Ironically, the sales orientation of Club Aluminum contributed to its inability to address these weaknesses and make appropriate changes. Selling requires positive thinking and an upbeat attitude. The background of Club's top leaders in sales reinforced this type of mentality; Taylor coined the term "R.M.A." for "right mental attitude," which he defined as "believing that what God wants done can be done." And when people deliberately choose to be positive, they often shut out "negative thinking." The result is that legitimate, helpful criticism is stifled, and hard-nosed analysis is passed over. When a particular product stops selling as well as it once did, the company tends to blame itself and its attitude rather than looking realistically at the product and the market.

Taylor was not dismayed by this critique. He welcomed suggestions for improvement, but he didn't fully grasp the scope of change that was necessary for Club Aluminum to grow. He understood what had made him successful, but he was losing touch with the shifting nature of meal preparation in the typical suburban household and, especially, with the contemporary women who now managed those households.

In 1960, the company invested in two further studies, one on the attitude of women toward aluminumware, and the other on Club Aluminum's public image. The Chicago-based Social Research firm did the analysis; their conclusions were sobering. Aluminum cookware and product lines, like Club Aluminum, were generally perceived by younger women as old-fashioned, traditional and suited for the serious cook, not the active housewife. Older women, both working class and middle class, still regarded Club Aluminum highly and were accustomed to responding to special promotions.

The newer housewife, however, did not share this loyalty. She was attracted to cookware that gave the impression of being technologically advanced (like stainless steel) as well as being attractive, lightweight and conducive to culinary experimentation. Few women took the time to analyze the differences between cookware metals. Advertising that appealed to modern tastes and high status guided their choices.

A more fundamental change was underway by 1960. The traditional role of the housewife was no longer held in high esteem. Three years later, Betty Friedan's *The Feminine Mystique* shattered the complacency of many suburban housewives who suddenly discovered how dull and bland their lives had become. A feminist movement was stimulated by Friedan's attack, yet change was evident even before her book appeared. More married women were entering the work force, and even those who chose to stay at home were busy with many community and school affairs. These women did not have the same amount of time their mothers did to prepare meals in the kitchen. Prepackaged dinners that could be heated up in the oven became more common, as did eating out at restaurants.

This did not mean that women were buying less cookware, but rather that they were choosing pots and pans that were easy to use and easy to clean. The more practical and efficient the products, the more likely they were to be purchased. Color and style were not insignificant factors either. The ceramic cookware produced by Corning Ware was gaining great popularity for these reasons, just as stainless steel had been doing for several years. (Unethical promoters of stainless steel were responsible for resurrecting worries about the safety of aluminum cookware, a fear that the Food and Drug Administration declared groundless in 1962.)

In 1960, the nonstick Teflon finish was introduced into the market. Cookware manufacturers, including Monarch, rushed to apply this nonporous resin to their pans. Two years later, Club Aluminum began selling their Black Magic line, a cast-aluminum fry pan with a Teflon finish inside. It proved to be a very successful item to merchandise, though not one without problems. The finish was easily scratched by sharp objects and scouring pads, and stains built up if the pan was not cleaned properly. Customers soon learned that Teflon finishes didn't last forever. Therefore, they didn't want to spend a lot of money on a frying pan. This was a disadvan tage for Club, whose products were always priced on the high end of the scale. Nevertheless, Club took advantage of the sensation to advertise on television during prime-time programming.

Teflon coatings captured a huge share of the cookware market during the early 60s, and was a boon for Club Aluminum, making up for the loss taken by their older lines (total sales volume had actually dropped badly in 1961 and 1962). But disappointment came when the American Stock Exchange delisted Club Aluminum because its volume of stock transactions was below minimum standards and because the market value of these shares was below $1 million. Taylor pleaded for special consideration given its years of good performance, but it was to no avail.

Serious cutbacks became necessary and the pressure to re-evaluate the leadership rose. Taylor surprised his management team by asking each of them to write him a memo saying what he would do if he were chief executive officer. Charlie Cecil boldly recommended that Taylor relinquish his post as CEO if he could not spend more time with the company. Taylor didn't take the suggestion but gave himself and all the other executives a twenty per cent pay cut. He then ordered a complete management review by the A. T. Kearney consultant firm.

The conclusions of this study recommended radical surgery, painful but effective. It urged liquidating Inland Glass Works, a move that was already underway after three unprofitable years selling carafes. It also proposed major reductions in expenses and more well-planned sales programs. The most crucial suggestion, however, was for Taylor to step down as CEO to be replaced by Allen Mathis.

Fortunately, Taylor was willing to make the move and glad to turn over the reins to his son-in-law. Ken Johnston took the opportunity to leave the company and became the president of the Metal Cookwares Association, a prestigious position in the industry and a recognition of his expertise and Club Aluminum's reputation among its competitors.

In the next five years, Club Aluminum regained its profitability though its position in the industry did not change. Cast-aluminum cookware could no longer compete against ceramic (also known as pyroceram) and stainless steel; a new process of lightweight, less-expensive drawn aluminum was also being tested for cookware manufacturing and threatened to undermine Club products.

Under Mathis's leadership, strategic reductions were made in the company's total operations. The rack-jobbing division which operated in East Coast supermarkets was sold. At the same time, Mathis took steps toward diversifying the product line by purchasing a kitchen-tool and a gadget manufacturer as well as the rights to sell an Irish-made, porcelain-enameled, cast-iron cookware especially designed for gourmet cooking. His goal was to capitalize on the Club name and reputation and increase the number of high-quality consumer-oriented products consistent with that image. The strategy helped to stabilize the company.

Taylor's role became very minimal in these years. He visited the office several days a week when he was in town and led a Bible study for interested employees.

The Selling of Club Aluminum

In 1966 Mathis left Club Aluminum to work for the American Management Association. He had gained a great appreciation for professional-management concepts while working at Club Aluminum and now had the opportunity to influence other executives. He became head of the AMA's President's Association, a corporate-executive training arm. Taylor was very pleased with this development and eagerly funneled Christian organizational executives into seminars led by Mathis, even underwriting the costs.

At that time Cecil became Club's president and continued in the same direction Mathis had started, diversifying and broadening the product lines. But Cecil's most momentous decision came in 1967 when he persuaded Taylor to sell his share of the stock to a third party who would also acquire Monarch. The objective was to merge the sales and manufacturing concerns under one management structure, presumably to be headed by Cecil.

Taylor's only requirements were that the new owners agree with and practice the same high, ethical standards Club Aluminum had and that all Club's employees be treated fairly in the transaction. Over the years Taylor had entertained countless offers to sell Club Aluminum. He almost always declined to even discuss the possibility, sensing that the priorities of the conglomerates were at odds with his.

Cecil, however, found a buyer whom Taylor could trust. John Bolton was the principal owner of Standard International, a conglomerate based in Andover, Massachusetts, and a financial backer of Billy Graham. Taylor and Bolton knew each other through their contacts with Graham.

Standard International was an unusual assortment of companies, to say the least. It began as a publisher and printer of Sunday-school curriculum and religious literature in Cincinnati, Ohio. Bolton then expanded into household cleaning products, surgical instruments and hospital supplies, steel joists and injection molding. In 1967, all of these various parts of Standard did a combined business of $58 million.

Bolton and his son-in-law, Dan Hogan, who actually functioned as the CEO, were ready to buy Club Aluminum and Monarch. Eddie Bloomberg of Monarch was also agreeable. The agreement was consummated on December 29, 1967. The next year Standard decided to move Club Aluminum to Cleveland, where the Monarch plant was located, and create a combined company called Club Products. Cecil was given the task of helping most of the Club employees find new jobs in the Chicago area. He did this successfully, to Taylor's delight. Ironically, Cecil himself did not remain as the CEO of the new Club Products. A misunderstanding with the Monarch executives created tensions for him, and he chose to take a position with another manufacturing company. For the remainder of his career, Cecil worked for several manufacturing firms, helping them through difficult periods. The influence of Taylor had made him a valuable asset in the industry.

Taylor was seventy-four years old when Club Aluminum's days ended. He never wrote an epitaph to his 37 years in the cookware business, but his personal satisfaction in a job well done was evident.

7

Billy Graham Crusade

Herbert Taylor's faith in Christ and his desire to share that faith with others grew as he entered the later years of his life. Indeed, rather than slowing down and resting on his laurels, Taylor actually engaged in his most aggressive evangelistic efforts after he passed his sixty-fifth birthday.

He told audiences he was working full-time for the Lord. He was, in fact, capitalizing on all the contacts and prestige accumulated over the years in order to accomplish some ambitious projects for God. Each of these was actually a sales campaign, but—instead of cookware—the product he was promoting was the gospel.

Billy Graham in the Windy City

The first and greatest of these endeavors was an evangelistic crusade in Chicago featuring Taylor's personal friend and admirer Billy Graham. The crusade held in 1962 proved to be a mammoth organizational undertaking. Several years were consumed planning for the three weeks of meetings at McCormick Place. Taylor was the driving force behind the Graham crusade. When it was over, Graham rightly called it "Herb Taylor's crusade."

For many years, Taylor had wanted to penetrate his tough, brawling city with the good news of forgiveness and salvation through Christ. He believed Chicago needed the Christian message as desperately as any city in the world; from his travels around the world, he also knew its bad reputation. His desire was for a "spiritual awakening" in Chicago, one that was led by dedicated Christian laymen and that permeated the civic life of the city.

Persuading Billy Graham to come to Chicago was the most difficult aspect of the entire experience. But there were few people, Graham included, who could resist Taylor once he was convinced that God had given him a plan.

Graham and Taylor were more than casual acquaintances. They first met each other when Graham was a young pastor in the Chicago suburb of Western Springs in the early 1940s. At that time, Graham had a radio program called "Songs in the Night," which he broadcast over Moody Bible Institute's station.

The rise of Youth for Christ in Chicago, especially with the huge rally in Soldier Field in 1945, launched Graham into his evangelistic career. Taylor was a financial backer and participant in those early YFC events; he assisted Chicago pastor Torrey Johnson in bringing together the various youth evangelists across the country that became the nucleus of Youth for Christ. Graham was the first full-time evangelist employed by YFC. He then traveled across the country, gaining national prominence in the 1950s through huge crusades in such major cities as New York.

The friendship between the two men deepened during these years and Graham often stayed in Taylor's home when he was in Chicago. The young evangelist was extremely impressed with Taylor's personal piety, calling him "one of the most committed and dedicated Christians I have ever known." Graham's fondness and respect for Taylor was not unlike a warm father-son relationship. When Taylor memorized the Sermon on the Mount and began reciting it daily, Graham followed his example. Graham also referred to Taylor's practice in his addresses and in conversations with business leaders.

Taylor began urging his friend to come to Chicago as early as 1954. Graham appeared to be interested, but there were other places to go, and Chicago loomed in his mind as an insurmountable obstacle. He felt like a prophet returning to his home town, and he honestly doubted that a successful crusade was possible in the religious climate of Chicago. "The Lord has certainly not given me a green light within my own heart," he told Taylor in 1959.

There were good reasons for Graham's reluctance. When the possibility of inviting Graham to Chicago was made public by Taylor and others, fundamentalist and liberal church leaders in the city spoke out against the idea. The fundamentalists, many of whom were linked with the Independent Fundamentalist Churches of America or the General Association of Regular Baptists, criticized Graham for cooperating with mainline Protestant churches in his crusades. They mistrusted his enormous success. Graham had diluted the gospel, they claimed, by not preaching strict separation from both worldliness and ecumenical affiliations. So vocal were these fundamentalists that even Moody Bible Institute hesitated in its support of Graham.

Liberal Protestants, on the other hand, were equally critical of Graham. Their organization, the Chicago Church Federation, was reluctant to support a crusade. They disliked Graham's old-fashioned "hellfire" preaching, the emotional altar calls and his evangelical theology. Taylor's own church in Park Ridge chose not to cooperate with Graham. Taylor was left with the task of organizing transportation to the meetings and recruiting church members to attend. (Fifteen people from the church were converted at the crusade, including the chairman of the religious-education board.)

Graham refused to conduct a crusade without solid church support. He told Taylor that key church leaders from all the denominations—conservative and liberal, White and Black—had to be recruited before he could even consider coming. He also mentioned the practical problem of a suitable place to conduct the meeting. Year by year the crowds attending his crusades had grown; there were few locations in Chicago which could handle 40,000 or more people every evening of the week.

Taylor was not dissuaded. He formed a committee of Christian laymen, all of them representing a different denomination. They spent time praying together and even met once with Graham to emphasize their desire that he come to Chicago. They then recruited other laymen, 300 in all, to join them in publicly calling for a Graham crusade in Chicago.

The next step was a vintage Taylor move. In the spring of 1960, he set up a breakfast meeting with Graham as the speaker and about 700 ministers in attendance, all individually invited by the 300 laymen. The goal was to persuade the ministers to publicly endorse a Graham crusade and, at the same time, to overcome Graham's reservations and doubts.

After Graham spoke, Taylor asked for a visible display of support. He began with the laymen. They all stood up to show their desire for a Graham crusade. Then Taylor put the same question to the ministers. They were on the spot, but all of them stood. Taylor was thrilled. He knew some of them had expressed their disagreement on earlier occasions, but now they were united. The consensus builder had managed to get 700 clergymen from numerous denominations to stand together and speak with one mind.

Then Taylor turned to Graham and put him in the same uncomfortable situation. The overwhelmed Graham could only promise to notify them of a decision in the near future. Taylor kept in close contact with Graham and, in his correspondence, spoke quite frankly about Graham's hesitation and his own conviction that God intended this crusade to be held in Chicago. Two weeks later, Graham agreed to come. The date was set for June 1962, which gave Taylor and his committee two years to prepare.

Taylor and his fellow laymen went to work. By then, they already knew they had a place where the crusade could be held, the new exposition center along Chicago's lakefront, called McCormick Place, which was to open in November 1960. Soldier Field, home of the Chicago Bears, was the logical choice for the climactic, final rally.

The administration of the crusade was to be an organiza-

tional masterpiece, unlike any Graham had enjoyed pre-
viously, but which would become a model for later evangelistic campaigns. An executive committee led by Taylor created a formidable array of subcommittees to oversee every
detail of the operation: publicity, fund-raising, counseling,
prayer support, ushering, hotel accommodations, transportation and security. Members of these committees were carefully selected from different churches to be sure all segments
of the Christian community were represented; in the end,
3,000 Chicago-area churches had some degree of participation in the crusade effort.

Taylor's influence was felt through all of these committees.
His confidence, poise and patience impressed many people
who were awed by the scope of a Graham crusade. One
executive-committee member told Taylor later, "Your business knowledge and acumen have been invaluable. The way
you made arrangements with difficult people, and got special
prices and considerations were wonderful to observe." Another member recalled a meeting when various problems
were discussed. Taylor suggested prayer and got down on his
knees. The others awkwardly followed him to the floor and
experienced the kind of humility that God always honors.

Taylor's skills were most evident in getting the army of
crusade workers to cooperate and serve on the same team.
Fundamentalists and liberals often found themselves on the
same committees. Black pastors mingled with their White
counterparts. Business leaders rubbed shoulders with clergy.
Relations were not always smooth, but Taylor's diplomacy
won out. He fulfilled exactly what Graham wanted from the
churches, and he also demonstrated the power of dedicated
laity in doing the Lord's work.

The crusade itself was a record-breaker. None of Graham's previous American crusades had attracted the numbers Chicago provided. The final service at Soldier Field drew 116,000 people, the largest audience to whom Graham had ever preached. Contributions came to more than $700,000, enough to pay all the bills and fund television replays of the crusade on 180 stations around the world. The most significant figure, however, was the 17,000 people who responded to Graham's invitation to follow Christ. Many of these converts ended up in Chicago churches.

The aftermath of the crusade was continued evangelistic outreach. Taylor and others on the executive committee incorporated themselves to conduct follow-up rallies with other evangelists, including Joe Blinco and Tom Skinner, and to promote the films produced by Graham's subsidiary, World-Wide Pictures. These efforts culminated in a second Graham crusade held in 1971. Taylor was the honorary chairman then, but he still devoted many hours of work, supporting men who had learned the mechanics of the Graham crusade from him back in 1962.

The Chicago Bible Society

During the 1960s, Taylor became actively involved with the Chicago Bible Society, an agency which distributed Bibles (or various books of the Bible) to hospital patients, prisoners and in various neighborhoods of Chicago. Businessmen like Taylor were recruited to help raise funds for the purchase of huge quantities of paperback portions of the Scriptures.

In 1965, as president of the society, Herbert Taylor helped launch a campaign to place one million copies of the Gospel of Mark in Chicago homes. Two years later he convinced the society to try a more unusual project. Taylor asked the Chicago Police Department to identify one of the most crime-infested neighborhoods in the city. The society then distributed 20,000 Bible portions with a coupon for a free Bible to that neighborhood. Bold members of the society even met with gangs in the neighborhood to give them Bibles in person. The goal was to reduce the crime rate. After some months, the police acknowledged that less crime had occurred though the exact connections were never explained.

Interestingly, Taylor's role with the Bible society got him into further trouble with hard-line fundamentalists. In 1967, a modern-language version of the New Testament (called *Good News for Modern Man*) was introduced and promoted by the society. Taylor even gave the society's Gutenberg Award in recognition of the key translator, Eugene Nida. This particular version of the Bible offended many fundamentalists who were tenaciously loyal to the King James Version and who suspected liberal influences in the Good News New Testament. Some even mounted campaigns against the modern-language version.

Taylor handled these attacks graciously. Ironically, he found himself criticized by fellow Methodists, including those he worshipped with every Sunday morning, for being too fundamentalist (a term he disliked very much). Yet, at the same time, fundamentalists were suspicious that he wasn't really a Bible-believing Christian. His strategy was to avoid theological squabbles and concentrate on positive action.

Living a Life of Faith

Earlier, when the National Association of Evangelicals (NAE) was attacked by right-wing fundamentalists during its early years, Taylor admonished NAE executives for fighting back. He said, "I have always found that when you have a controversy on your hands, it is better to walk into the other fellow's camp, find out where he is vulnerable and attempt to sell him on your point of view." It was precisely this attitude that marked the new evangelical style which helped to set aside the traditional type of feisty fundamentalism.

His way of identifying a Christian was far more pragmatic. "My concern is with the visible aspect of being a Christian," he wrote in his autobiography. True Christians demonstrated in their lives what they claimed to be. Taylor looked for such things as confession of faith in Christ as Savior, regular Bible reading, acts of love toward others, tithing, a role in evangelism of some kind, and personal qualities like cheerfulness, patience and humility.

His Christian yardstick was not unlike the Four-Way Test. Both his faith and his ethics were to be applied in daily situations, not debated or discussed in abstract terms. He rarely read books about the Bible; the Bible itself was enough. Nevertheless, his theological convictions were quite conservative (as a trustee at Fuller Seminary, he became uncomfortable with more progressive faculty members). His desire to achieve results and his inclination to avoid offending others kept him from arguing about doctrinal issues.

The Methodist Church

Only in his activities as a Methodist did Taylor attempt to push his theological views. His loyalty to the denomination of his youth never wavered, though he was decidedly unhappy about the trends in that church. He held back funds for small, struggling Methodist churches in the Chicago area because he wasn't convinced the ministers were preaching "a real gospel message." Several overtures from Northwestern University President James A. James to join the board of trustees were rejected, as were requests from Garrett Biblical Institute for scholarship funds. (Taylor only became generous when he was assured that the students were conservative.) He even voiced his concern to the denominational publishing house for its lack of "evangelistic emphasis" in church-school literature.

While never hostile or belligerent, Taylor grew increasingly ardent in his zeal for a Bible-based, traditional faith, and he yearned for its restoration in the denomination of his youth. Any organized efforts to promote Bible reading and teaching appealed to him, as did campaigns to distribute Bibles.

Taylor was not alone in this concern. By the 1950s, many Methodists were expressing alarm at the widespread ignorance of biblical teaching and history among the laity. The devotional guide *The Upper Room* became a successful antidote to this biblical illiteracy.

His friendship with Ford Philpott, a Methodist evangelist, was also an indication of his denominational loyalties. Taylor was as close to Philpott as he was to Graham. Through Philpott, he helped organize men's Bible-study groups in many Methodist congregations.

By the early 1970s, Taylor was convinced "the fires of evangelism are again starting to sweep through this great church." He chaired a denominational committee on evangelism. Together with another conservative Methodist, Stanley Kresge, he organized an evangelical Methodist caucus in 1970 which became the Good News Movement. Unfortunately, Taylor did not live to see the effects of this movement on the entire church.

The apostle Paul described evangelism as a team operation. Some Christians plant the seed, some water the ground and nurture the plant, while others harvest the crop. Taylor did all three of these functions at different times in his career. Most of the time, however, he performed the essential behind-the-scenes work that allowed articulate spokesmen for the gospel to win many converts. He left behind an astounding legacy of evangelistic organizations that to this day continue to spread the word and bring people to Christ.

8

Final Days: A Legacy of Ministry

I believe that everybody whom the Lord uses is going to be faced with hardships," Herbert Taylor once said. "These are for our good. Sometimes through answers to prayer the Lord will deliver us from them. On other occasions we have to go through the testing."

Much of Taylor's testing came at the end of his life, after he suffered a debilitating stroke. His final years were a marked contrast to the incredibly busy career he had maintained almost to his eightieth birthday. He became an invalid, confined to his home in Park Ridge and totally dependent on Gloria. His physical decline did not diminish his spirit or his confidence in God, however. He remained a man who "glowed," as one of his daughters said.

The stroke occurred in 1975. It resulted in aphasia, a disability which causes the loss of speech and the ability to communicate. In effect, Taylor lost almost his entire vocabulary. His mind functioned, but he had no way to articulate his thoughts. He could only speak a few words. Often aphasia also affects the personality, usually causing a person to withdraw from people. For Taylor, that was not the case: he was still the same friendly, jovial man. Outwardly, he was dignified, cooperative and in control of himself.

He enjoyed taking daily walks in the neighborhood by himself to keep up his strength. He was very diligent about practicing his word therapy daily. Some days he would put Bible-reading records on the record player and listen intently. More important to his morale were six friends from his men's Bible study at church, who often came to take him out to lunch. One of these friends, who had himself recovered from aphasia, took a special interest in his therapy, coming every week to his home.

Gloria and Herb attended church regularly and were still able to travel together to visit their children in Alabama and New Jersey. As difficult as it was for Gloria and the rest of the family to not hear him speak, they drew close to him. Gloria, Ramona and Beverly spent hours helping him learn to talk again by using flash cards with pictures of simple objects. A man who had loved children and youth so much during his life was now at the dependency level of a child himself.

The daughters took time from their own schedules to help their mother; they took walks with their father, went out for dinner with him, and listened to records together. He also spent time with his daughters' families, enjoying time with his grandchildren. (Just before he died, his first great-grand-child, Herbert Taylor Hargrave, was born.)

Beverly and Ramona could only guess what was going on inside of him. What they saw on his face was contentment, joy, peace. Both were convinced that all the Scripture he had memorized and recited daily was refreshing his soul, an investment of time now paying off rich rewards. In spite of his disablties, Taylor radiated the presence of God.

He left his broken body behind on May 1, 1978, to meet the God whom he had given a lifetime to serve. He died with few regrets and little unfinished business. Like the apostle Paul, he had run the race to the very end. He had followed God's plan for his life as best he understood it—and he understood it better than most.

There were tears at his funeral at the Methodist church in Park Ridge, but the crowd in the sanctuary shared a warm affection for him and a deep satisfaction for a life well spent. George Beverly Shea sang some of Taylor's favorite hymns. Ford Philpott, Don Hoke and LeRoy Patterson all gave tribute to their departed friend.

Few men or women are blessed with the energy, dedication and vision which Taylor possessed. Few have the opportunities to make an impact on a world scale. God gave him much, expected much and received much. God took home a "good and faithful servant."

Postscript to a Career

Though Taylor has been gone for more than a decade, his work continues on. The many projects he started are now being carried out by others. Almost all the organizations he launched are still functioning, most of them thriving. The many individuals who claimed him as a mentor and example of godliness have passed on to others what they learned from him. Taylor left a remarkable legacy.

The Four-Way Test is still an important feature of almost every Rotary club around the world. Many clubs have committees to find ways to promote its use in the community. Plaques, posters and signs are still being posted for workers, drivers and students to see and apply.

Taylor's granddaughter, Caryl Lynn Cusick, oversees the work of the Four-Way Test Association, a non-profit organization based in Montgomery, Alabama. Its purpose is to promote the Test and provide educational materials and gift items displaying the four questions.

Club Aluminum, re-named Club Products, was eventually sold in 1984 by Standard International to Regal Ware, a Wisconsin-based cookware manufacturer. By then, the Club plant had been relocated from Cleveland to Jacksonville, Arkansas, where it continues to operate today. There are over 200 employees in the company with several different product lines and divisions. Cast-aluminum cookware is still the mainstay of the enterprise. The home-party plan has been revived and even used in Great Britain with some degree of success. Taylor's name is hardly remembered in the offices and warehouses of the current Club Products. Yet the company still makes and sells what Taylor recognized in 1930 as high-quality cookware.

The Christian Worker's Foundation also continues to function. Mathis left the American Management Association in the late 1960s to become a professional corporate director; both Allen and Beverly live in Alabama. Ramona and Bob Lockhart spent most of their years in New Jersey, where Bob was an executive in the food industry. For a brief period of time, he was a director of Club Aluminum. For him, Taylor was a strong Christian example, a man who brought him closer to God by demonstrating what the Christian life was like.

Taylor's seven grandchildren (Beverly and Allen have two daughters and one son; Ramona and Bob have two daughters and two sons) are all grown, married and some have children of their own. "The bottom line is they know the Lord," said Ramona. Success in a career is always secondary, though it often follows commitment to God.

Fortunately, the third generation also knew their grandfather and received a glimpse of his character and love for children. Taylor wrote letters to each of them as they reached important milestones in their lives. His words to them were always encouraging and challenging. He rewarded them for memorizing the Four-Way Test and Scripture passages. In later years, he visited them for short periods of time and watched them perform in sports and music. He was the perfect grandfather, complete with old-fashioned, pince-nez glasses perched on his nose, right above a ready smile and just below a twinkling eye.

But how should those who never knew Taylor remember him? What, beyond his amazing accomplishments, should be kept in our collective memory on which to reflect from time to time? Simply this: Herbert J. Taylor lived according to a set of values which he drew from the Bible and on which he built his whole life. These values are what we must remember. These we can reaffirm for ourselves.

Wealth, prestige or power never defined success for Taylor. Rather, success was using the talents God gave you in the way he intended them to be used. "Realize that you are you," he often told students. "Whatever you choose to do in life eventually should be in accord with your own thoughts, interests and talents and in accordance with God's will for you.

"Many people today are locked into occupations that do not satisfy them at all, because they didn't take time to analyze intelligently what their true talents and interests were when they were younger, or because they sacrificed a chance to do work that they liked, for work that offered more immediate financial gain. It is a tragedy to look upon our work as a void that takes its toll of time and strength and gives nothing in return but wages!"

He also said, "When we have determined what our true talents are, have dedicated them to a single worthwhile cause, have realized that they are a gift from God and not to be accepted lightly or without responsibility, we can overcome obstacles and adverse circumstances. Success won't come overnight. It takes patience and hard work, perhaps even bitter experiences that will test every bit of endurance we have. But, if we have chosen wisely in the beginning—not been influenced by all the temptations to take 'just any job' to get a car or clothes, spending money for dates—we have approached the problem intelligently and will select work we can do well and that will give us happiness and strength to see it through to a successful conclusion.

"When you know what God has given you, you will know what you can give the world, and you will know the paths to true happiness and contentment for both you and your family."

If you pressed Taylor further about knowing what God had given you to do, he would have directed you to the Bible. There you find principles by which to guide your decisions and encouragement to appreciate your own unique qualities and gifts. In this connection, he kept telling people, "God has a plan for you." That plan for the individual fit into his larger plan for the world. "I am quite certain that God has a part for each one of us in his plans for the solution of these problems, so let us humbly ask him where, when and how he can use us and then follow his will for us."

Another value to which he held tenaciously was service to others, meeting other people's needs, unselfishly caring for someone else. This too he found in the Bible. In God, he found the source of this kind of love, a love that reached out in friendship.

Taylor's mission field for this biblical ideal of service was Rotary International. Among businessmen, professionals and statesmen, he articulated a way of life which grew out of the Sermon on the Mount, his daily spiritual food. Though he was careful in choosing his words, he never held back in promoting Christ's commands of love for others. Under his leadership, Rotary became a friendship-builder, a creator of good will, an agent of peacemaking between people from all nations, races and religious backgrounds.

A third value dear to Taylor was the control and discipline of his mind. "As a man thinketh in his heart, so is he" was one of his favorite proverbs. He urged the young people to whom he spoke to train their minds—by getting as much education as possible, applying what they knew to problems they faced, and then submitting their minds to God's plan.

"A person with wholesome, disciplined thoughts stands on the threshold of understanding God's plan for his life," he said. "This, by far, is the most valuable service the mind can render. In the complicated world of today's adult, with pressures and philosophies attacking him from all quarters, fortunate are the men or women who can face the complexities and contradictions and see God's plan for them clearly."

None of these values can be considered profound or original. They have a folksy, down-to-earth practicality, the typical advice that older generations give to the younger who often aren't listening. But few people actually lived out these values as well as Taylor. His example gave his words immense credibility.

As a Christian who spent most of his time in the business world, Taylor's effort to translate what he learned in the Bible to the relationships of the marketplace is especially credible. Over a decade ago writer Bill Krutza probed the "nearsighted ethics" of many Christian businessmen. He wrote in the September 1976 issue of *Eternity:*

> We can give multitudes of stories to illustrate the difference between what we call Christian men in business and what we would like to see—Christian businessmen.
>
> What makes the difference? Is it possible to find the truly Christian businessman?
>
> To answer these questions, and to form some type of Christian perspective, let us go back to that rather simplistic formula: profit, products, people and principles. Quite obviously we have concluded this is the wrong order.
>
> One must first of all have a clear understanding of Christian principles. These can only come by a systematic study of the New Testament, especially the life of Jesus Christ.
>
> And then how do we treat people? How does the love of neighbor affect business decisions? What about the integrity of the individual, the value Jesus Christ placed upon

personhood? What about a person's creative abilities? Jesus Christ had a deep respect for the worth of each individual, so much so he stopped to minister to each regardless of the person's status or need. So much so that he died for individuals and brings the benefits of his atoning death to people on a one by one basis.

We must start here. Principles governing the life of each person. Then the principles of Christian interpersonal relationships. These deal with honesty, justice, fair play, returning good for evil, creative use of other people's talents, the eternal worth of people and ideas.

When we thus encourage and promote the creativity of people with whom we work, there's little worry that the products will not be forthcoming. Motivated by a sense of personal worth, people will produce abundantly. Once this happens, the profits will fall in line.

He could well have spoken of Herbert Taylor as just this kind of Christian businessman.

Bibliographical Note

This biography was written for Herbert Taylor's friends and those who wish to be acquainted with the creator of the Four-Way Test, the founder of the Christian Worker's Foundation and the president of Club Aluminum. For this reason, footnotes have been omitted. The goal was to discover the real man, not just an historical character.

The sources, however, should be acknowledged. Most of the quotations in this account can be found in Mr. Taylor's autobiography, *God Has a Plan for You* (Fleming Revell, 1968). A later edition appeared under the title *The Herbert J. Taylor Story* (Downers Grove, Ill.: InterVarsity Press, 1968). Several of his speeches were published as booklets, including *If I Were 21*. I quoted from these as well.

Taylor was a prolific letter writer. Fortunately, he kept copies of everything and filed them carefully. He even preserved scrawled notes to himself and stored them. The Club Aluminum papers, the foundation papers and his Rotary papers were all rich treasures to examine. His correspondence with friends like Billy Graham gave intimate insights into Taylor's piety. Reading this material was similar to reading a diary.

Several texts provided me with important background information. Earl Lifshey's *The Houseware Story: A History of the American Housewares Industry* (National Houseware Manufacturers Association, 1973) was a great help. So was J. Fred MacDonald's *Don't Touch That Dial: Radio Programming in American Life from 1920 to 1960* (Chicago: Nelson-Hall, 1979).

Taylor was one of the noted "dollar-a-year" men during World War II. Donald Nelson tells their story in *Arsenal of Democracy* (New York: Harcourt, Brace & Company, 1946).

Business, Religion and Ethics, edited by Donald Jones (Cambridge: Delgeschlager, Gunn & Hain, 1982), is a fine collection of essays. Doug Sherman's *Your Work Matters to God* (Colorado Springs: Navpress, 1988) is worth reading in this connection. I refer to both books in this biography.

The story of Rotary International has been told many times. A booklet, *Panorama of a Half Century,* was published for the Golden Anniversary year in 1955 and gives highlights of each year since Paul Harris started the first club in 1905. Various publications about Rotary can be obtained through their international offices at 1 Rotary Center, Evanston, Illinois 60201. Four-Way Test materials can be ordered from the Four-Way Test Association, 4211 Carmichael Road, Montgomery, Alabama 36106.

George Marsden's *Reforming Fundamentalism* (Grand Rapids: Eerdmans, 1988) relates the history of Fuller Theological Seminary and mentions Taylor's role in its founding. *The Growth of a Work of God* by C. Stacey Woods (Downers Grove, Ill.: InterVarsity Press, 1978) and *Young Life* by Emile Cailliet (New York: Harper & Row, 1963) are personal accounts of two youth organizations launched by Taylor. My history of Christian Service Brigade, *The Brigade Trail* (Christian Service Brigade, 1987), devotes an entire chapter to Taylor.

The Four-Way Test

Today, the Four-Way Test is used by and on the desks of approximately 800,000 business and community leaders in 51 countries around the world. It has been placed on monuments and billboards. It is on the walls of schools, libraries, factories and business offices. In the USA it has been adopted by state and city legislatures and has been the inspiration for several large civic and community-wide campaigns in Dallas, Texas; Daytona Beach, Florida; Pittsburgh, Pennsylvania to name a few.

The Four-Way Test Association, a non-profit organization, was founded in 1959 to promote the use of the Four-Way Test. The association works to provide resource materials, instruction, speakers and consultants to individuals and groups—introducing and encouraging its use in schools, governments, businesses and homes as a yardstick for building better communications and stronger, more effective relationships between people. *A catalog of materials promoting the Four-Way Test is available through the association at 4211 Carmichael Road, Montgomery, AL 36106, or call (205) 277-6390.*

In business, civic life, at home . . . the Four-Way Test speaks its practicality. It helps individuals to think beyond immediate desires, to consider the consequences of actions and not focus on what is merely expedient. The Four-Way Test acts as a lubricant that smooths personal relations by basing them on truth and consideration for others.

The Four-Way Test . . . of What We Think, Say or Do
1. Is it the TRUTH?
2. Is it FAIR to All Concerned?
3. Will it Build GOODWILL and Better Friendships?
4. Will it Be BENEFICIAL to All Concerned?

Marketplace Ministry

Jesus didn't call just clergy to build his church. He called people in the marketplace. He lived in a country crowded with seminary graduates. Yet not one of Jesus' twelve, original disciples was a Sadducee, Pharisee, prophet or priest. Instead, he chose to build his church with a handful of entrepreneurs. Independent business-men whose only theological education came from the school of hard knocks.

God's Word is more than a guide for the church. It's a manual for the marketplace. In a church that depends so heavily on clergy, Bible studies tend to be colored by a clerical point of view. We love to spotlight spiritual giants—the great priests and prophets of their day. But the Bible is full of people just like you. In fact, a full 75 per cent of all the major characters in God's Word never held a religious job in their lives. Somehow, we've forgotten that time after time—from Daniel to Nehemiah, from Esther to Lydia—God called everyday people to be his workaday ministers in the real world. And he still does.

Evangelism isn't a Sunday experience. It's an everyday part of life in the marketplace. What could be a more natural ministry for the average person than sharing your faith with a friend? Yet we've come to depend on specialists to do it for us. By way of the altar call. Or the evangelistic rally. Thank goodness the Scriptures are filled with alternate ways to deliver the good news—opportunities that grow as a matter of course out of our everyday relationships, allowing us to share the gospel with candor and freedom.

Work is not a necessary evil; it's a necessary ministry in the marketplace. What it all boils down to is this: The clergy are called to serve the church. But the laypeople *are* the church. This was the rallying cry of the Reformation: that all believers are his priests. And everything we do is sacred in his sight. We must learn to see our work as a calling, not just a means to an end. It is through work that we reflect his image as the creator, the master craftsman of the world around us.

That's why we created the Marketplace ministry. To help workaday people learn to live their faith effectively. And to make sure that America's young people—the next generation of marketplace Christians—discover what it means to be his ministers in the real world. Seven days a week.

Make no mistake—we don't cut paychecks to a large cadre of full-time ministers. Instead, we are purely and simply an informal network for the sharing of resources.

Products in the marketplace. Already the Marketplace vision has been translated into a remarkable variety of tangible tools. First and foremost is *Marketplace Networks,* a newsletter rich with articles, interviews, news, reviews and Bible studies of special concern to Christians in the marketplace. We will also be creating a radio program, producing audio and video cassettes, publishing books, Sunday-school programs, and even a special Marketplace Study Bible—all designed to help transform your everyday routine into a dynamic ministry in the marketplace.

People in the marketplace. Across the country, Marketplace sponsors regular student/lay leader gatherings to help searching young people understand that even the most ordinary vocation is filled with spiritual opportunity. We also sponsor other programs as the need arises—everything from "Theology of Laity" conferences to gatherings of Christian guilds.

In other words, wherever Christians are working to fulfill the Marketplace mission, we'll be working hard to support them. And we want you to know that we covet your participation. And your prayers.

For more information write:

Marketplace
6400 Schroeder Road/P.O. Box 7895
Madison, WI 53707-7895